OREO

RACE and

MARGINAL MEN and WOMEN

by
Charles V Willie, PhD
Professor of Education and Urban Studies
Graduate School of Education
Harvard University

$A \dashv3 \int \infty \diamond \equiv | \cap \Omega$
PARAMETER PRESS, INC
705 Main Street, Wakefield, Massachusetts 01880
United States

Library of Congress Catalog Card Number 74-24480
International Standard Book Number 0-88203-006-X

Printed and bound in the United States of America by
The Murray Printing Company
Forge Village, Massachusetts 01828

Composition by
Parameter Press, Inc
Wakefield, Massachusetts 01880

Dedicated to the

memory of

MARTIN LUTHER KING, JR

and

MARTIN BUBER

who tried to reconcile

the peoples of this world

TABLE OF CONTENTS

PREFACE

This book examines the role and responsibility of marginal people in society, especially with respect to race relations. It is an analysis of social change and the contributions to this process by black men and women who live in, between, and beyond their race. They are disparagingly referred to as *oreos*, but in the end they may be society's heros who willingly sacrifice short-range personal security for long-range social survival. They help collectivities and clans find just and loving ways of cooperating with each other for their mutual benefit.

New strategies in race relations are discussed. They transcend the segregationist movement of whites and the separatist movement of blacks. Reconciliation may not be a popular proposal, but ultimately it is the only plan that will work.

This book is, in part, a statement of the author's personal involvement in conflict situations and his attempt to put into practice the principles of sociology. One could call it a book about *doing* sociology in specific situations, particularly those involving race. It begins with an example of creative conflict—the case of the Oreo cookie at the Hood College Conference, then examines the sources of personal identity, interaction between the person and society, and how institutions influence individuals. Blacks are described as marginal people in the New World with a mission not unlike that of Jewish people in the Old World. Discussions on power and participation, pluralism and interdependence are followed by an overview of racial hatred and reconciliation from an international perspective. The book ends with an analysis and interpretation of the funeral and festival for Martin Luther King, Jr, an excellent example of a marginal man.

The author is most grateful to Jane Keddy, president of Parameter Press, who is a friend as well as a publisher and who gently nurtured this project to completion. Her life has been one of creative marginality, which is what this book is all about.

The text departs from the usual rhetoric of race relations and tries to present a different perspective that is personal and yet professional. It may be of interest to students of race as well as for the study of conflict and change.

C V W
February 14, 1975

CHAPTER 1

OREO
— MARGINAL MAN AND WOMAN
ON TRIAL

The Oreo cookie became for me a "piece of finite reality," in the words of Paul Tillich. It was a bearer of something beyond itself; it was the medium for a holy encounter, "a medium of revelation" [Tillich 1955, pp 22-24].* The Oreo cookie is a thick, double chocolate wafer with white cream filling in the middle. The coloring is brown and white and brown again.

LIKE IT IS IN THE WASHINGTON PROVINCE

In mid-June of 1969 at Hood College in Frederick, Maryland, the Washington Province of the Episcopal Church convened its annual conference. The Washington Province includes all or parts of the states of Pennsylvania, West Virginia, Delaware, Maryland, Virginia, and the District of Columbia. The theme for the conference was, "Like It Is and Like It Will Be." I was engaged as the morning lecturer to tell it like it is. The Rev Herbert J Ryan, S J, had the responsibility of forecasting how it will be.

It was not my morning lectures, however, that were the turning point for the conference. Rather, the Oreo cookie

---

*At the back of the book is a list of References which gives full information about the works of authors cited in brackets.

emerged as a symbol both of racial separation and of racial integration at the Hood Conference. What happened demonstrated that actions speak louder than words. It is for this reason that I have urged many who call themselves religious, compassionate, humane, or civilized to focus as much upon actions as upon attitudes.

Let us get on with the story and the unfolding events. I was invited to be the morning lecturer for the conference. My wife, Mary Sue, and I arrived on the tree-lined campus of Hood College on a hot and humid Sunday afternoon in time for dinner and the Sunday evening Eucharist.

In terms of our conventional way of classifying people, I am black and my wife is white. In the Washington Province of the Episcopal Church, especially at a conference in Frederick, Maryland, race is always a significant variable, particularly when it involves male and female. I tell you these facts because they are related to the symbol of the Oreo cookie and the racial encounter which it mediated.

Early Monday morning at 8:30 AM I began my lecture by outlining a series of five topics related to the conference theme. The proposed series included (1) The Twofold Mission of the Church in the World, (2) Impediments to Effective Church Action, (3) The Interdependent Community, (4) The Anticommunity Force: Separatism, and (5) The Black Manifesto: A Strange Cry for Redemption, an Urgent Call for Repentance. The actual topics and sequence of lectures were changed following the episode of the Oreo cookie midway through the conference.

SWEET HARMONY EVAPORATES

In addition to the 45-minute lecture each morning, the conference was organized into several institutes that met daily and dealt with special subjects like church music, politics, revolution in the church, black and white relations, and Christian education. Each institute had a regular leader and visiting lecturers. The institute on black and white relations generated a great deal of anxiety. On the one hand, there was the coming together of black and white people to discuss America's most obvious failure, our own inability to get along with persons of different races; and, on the other hand, there was the coming together of younger and older people, trying to do business with each other in spite of the generation gap. This institute bore the burden of the racial and age separations and their characteristic estrangements.

I might add that the entire conference confessed its fault on the matter of age segregation and did something about it. Younger people—high school youth and young adults—were not separated from the main conference as in the past. They were part of the mainstream and participated in all the sessions.

For more than twenty years, the Hood Conference has been racially integrated. In fact, the conference was moved from Virginia to Maryland a few decades ago so that black and white people could attend. The conference included men and women, although men were a minority of all participants.

The conference opened with the components of an explosive America interacting as if they were defused. In time, sweet harmony evaporated and exposed the divisions that persisted.

By Wednesday morning, I had worked my way through the topics about church mission and the impediments to church action. A warm appreciative applause followed each lecture. The meaning of such action is never clear. Is one being thanked for entertaining the audience, for confirming individuals' existing ideas, for not upsetting the people, or for telling it like it is? The Wednesday morning reaction was very much like that of the days before. But the substance of my lecture was a bit different. In addition to an analysis of the current social situation, I expressed a series of judgments:

≫1. that the most important capacity to cultivate in the professional leadership of the church is the capacity to develop, maintain, and enhance community;

≫2. that a worshiping congregation that is a worshiping community must deliberately draw all sorts and conditions of people into the fellowship of the faithful; and

≫3. that the continued existence of all-white and all-black congregations is a blasphemous tragedy of contemporary civilization.

All this was said Wednesday morning in a lecture on the Interdependent Community.

By Wednesday noon, the divisions had emerged and were rotating on a black-white axis that intersected in the dining hall after lunch. An announcement over the public address system was made by a black priest. He said in jest that a revolution was about to start and that a black caucus was to be held in the end of the dining hall immediately after lunch. The purpose for the black caucus was not stated publicly. Later, someone said that it was called to recommend black candidates for the Board of Directors of the Hood Conference. However, the caucus never got down to business. Shortly after the caucus met, it was dismissed by the clergyman who had announced the assembly. His act of dismissal was an action of wisdom as argument began between black and white people who were present.

WHY CRASH THE BLACK CAUCUS?

The first person to crash the black caucus was a white woman whose husband is a priest who was scheduled to serve a predominantly black congregation. I suppose this is why she went to the caucus. Earlier, after the morning lecture, I had talked with this white conference member about her personal concerns and worries surrounding the new venture that she and her husband were about to undertake. I talked with her about the impossibility of avoiding mistakes; about the capacity which people have to forgive, especially the capacity of people who have been oppressed. I said that, once she had been forgiven for a mistake, the basis for a real relationship would be laid. I then wished her well in her new involvement with a different kind of parish life in a predominantly black community. I suppose this white conference member felt she belonged in the black caucus. A few black people did not see it that way; they did not know of her circumstances. It might not have mattered even if they had known who she was and what her husband was about to do. So they demanded that she leave. She insisted that she must stay. This was only the first argument. Others were to follow immediately.

When I had been at lunch, a white tablemate insisted that the calling of the black caucus was discrimination and wanted to know what to do about it. I said, in conversation at the table, that black people and any people have the right to withdraw and that white people and any people have the right to pursue the withdrawn if their pursuit is based on love, is an expression of genuine need for others, is a desire to share their burdens, and is an attempt to fulfill their needs. I provided some information that I had recently learned about two black men at the conference—a layman and a clergyman from Pennsylvania.

They had attended nearly twenty of these conferences in the past. In fact, the summer conference of the Washington Province of the Episcopal Church had been moved to Hood College largely because of the hot pursuit of these two men and other black people who knew that they were interdependent with white people and needed the experience of a summer church conference. It was because they had persisted in applying for admission to the all-white summer conferences more than twenty years before that Hood Conference is now interracial.

Thus the separatist movement among whites within the church, I explained, had been broken up by blacks who knew that the world was interdependent and that they and the whites needed each other. I then suggested that the separatist movement among blacks would be ended only if whites could admit that they needed blacks and therefore would pursue them in a spirit of love and interdependence.

Such pursuits were risky, I cautioned my listeners. The result might be that whites would experience some of the same kinds of insults that blacks had experienced years ago as they pursued whites who had insisted on maintaining racially segregated organizations and who openly stated that blacks were unwanted. Now blacks are saying similar things. Now whites must make a similar move for interdependence, a move that is based on love but that involves a risk to personal comfort.

Lunch was finished and the conversation ended. My wife and I arose to go to the black caucus, not knowing that another white person was already there. We did not issue the invitation, but two other white women from our luncheon table decided to go to the caucus with us. I don't know if they were with fear; but one woman was literally trembling.

WHOSE PROBLEM WAS IT?

The call for a caucus along racial lines was a call that created a problem. But whose problem was it—the problem of a black and white couple or the problem of a black or white caucus? In the Scriptures it is written, ". . . a man shall leave his father and mother and be joined to his wife, and the two shall become one" [Ephesians 5:31]. "What therefore God hath joined together, let not man put asunder" [Matthew 19:6], not even a black or white caucus. Where I go, there also may go my wife as we cleave to each other as one flesh.

But some members of the caucus didn't see it that way. The question is: Does family unity take precedence over racial unity? My wife and I affirm that it does.

So we approached the black caucus hand in hand. Attention focused on us as we approached the caucus, whose members were standing at one end of the dining hall.

"What are you doing here!" someone shouted at my wife.

"She is my wife!" I responded.

Then attention was turned to the two white women who came with us.

"Why are they here!" said the crowd.

"They are my friends!" I retorted.

"They have no right to be here!" was the angry reply.

"They are human beings," I said. "This is a caucus of human beings; let's get on with the meeting!"

One black man yelled that the humanity of whites was a debatable point. I told him that such a conception of race and humanity was his problem, not ours. Later I learned that the man who questioned the humanity of whites in the heat of argument is a clergyman. As the exchange became more intense, the other clergyman, who had convened the caucus, sensed a deteriorating situation.

"Caucus dismissed," he declared.

THE SIGN ON THE SHEET

By accident, chance, or intuition, I already had announced the topic for the next day—a discussion of the Black Manifesto. The topic had been shifted from Friday to Thursday. Moreover, I had requested that the Manifesto and the Response of the Executive Council of the Episcopal Church to the Manifesto be duplicated so that all might read them overnight. My plan was to distribute these documents after dinner.

Mine was not the only after-dinner plan. Someone decided to retaliate for the noontime confrontation. A sign on a sheet had been painted, a sign about the conference morning speaker. It read,

DR WILLIE IS AN OREO COOKIE

Beside these words was the likeness of that cookie—dark brown (or black) on the outsides and white on the inside. The sign then suggested a course of action; it called for a boycott of the Thursday morning lecture. The sign was positioned above the door to the hall in which the evening lecture was to be presented. The sheet sheltered the doorway like a curtain so that all had to pull it aside to go through, so that all would be encouraged to read it.

The idea for the sign came from a young black woman who lived in the District of Columbia. At the time, I did not know her. First I read the sign. Then I inquired about who its author was. I wanted to meet the person who was that unhappy with me. I wanted to know why that person was displeased. Also I wanted to defend my actions and to explain the feelings that I had. But the author of the sign did not come forward until an annoyed conference member ripped it down.

Meanwhile, as the sign danced in the breeze, my wife and I retaliated. We stood behind the sign by the doorway and handed out documents for the next day's session, copies of the Black Manifesto and of the Response by the Executive Council of the Episcopal Church. We could have distributed these documents elsewhere in the building. But we decided to confront the sign if not its author and to overcome what was supposed to be an insult. Our presence and the sign were excitement. It was clear that the noontime drama had not ended. Indeed, the tension was escalating, and the outcome was in doubt.

My wife drew courage and strength from the adverse situation and determined that events should run their full course. Thus she held high the sign of the Oreo cookie for late arrivals to see, since it had been pulled down earlier by a conference participant. I continued to hand out the documents. The intended insult was becoming a farce. This was too much for the author to tolerate. She came forth and snatched the banner from the hands of my wife, insisting that it was her property. My wife was hurt by this act of hostility and rejection and momentarily lost her composure. She was comforted by other conference members and made a rapid recovery.

THE DESIRE FOR SEPARATISM

The designer of the sign, having revealed herself, was pursued by me for questioning. She was an attractive black teenager from Washington. I wanted to find out her reasons for insisting on racial separation. I tried to set forth some points in favor of integration. I became adamant in discussing the right of my wife to be with me no matter what coloring any caucus might be. The young woman spoke of the need for black people to be alone so that they could find their own identity. I informed the sign maker that her separatist ideology could lead to a bloody end that she might not be prepared to experience, for only by violence would my wife and I be separated. Those who insist on calling racial caucuses must be prepared to accept the inseparable couples whose members might be of different races. I wanted to impress upon this young person that the call for segregation was not a game. An adult black woman stood with the youthful conference member as we talked. She allowed that a white wife of a black husband should be accepted, but she insisted that other whites should have left the black caucus when they were ordered to do so. She termed "arrogant" their arguments against leaving.

To provide historical perspective, I pointed out that the Washington Province Conference probably was very uncomfortable when blacks insisted on attending years ago. I explained that, because blacks had insisted on disturbing whites out of their comfortable segregation in the past, the possibility for an interracial confrontation was present today. I concluded that blacks who insisted on maintaining segregation must now expect to be made similarly uncomfortable, for the world and its people are interdependent. None can make it on his or her own. Shortly thereafter, the evening session began with Father Ryan leading the discussion. We had to break off our conversation unfinished.

THE NEED FOR SOLITUDE AND THE KNOCK ON THE DOOR

I worked hard that night on the next morning's lecture. It would be difficult to heal the broken hearts, especially since my behavior was a factor in the estrangement. Someone was needed to provide a perspective. I considered this to be my major task. Some black youth were bitter about the black caucus that had been crashed by whites. Some white adults were angered and insulted by the language used by blacks in the Manifesto. My responsibility was to deal with both issues in a way that would be helpful to all. My mission was nearly impossible. Yet I thought I should give it a try.

I read, I thought, and I wrote. I wished desperately for solitude and serenity to help the process of meditation and the sorting out of feeling from fact.

Suddenly there was a knock at my door. I answered. There stood a white youth, seeking me out in behalf of his friends. My thought and preparation were interrupted as I accepted his summons to come to the basement below to meet with a group of white teenagers.

They wanted to talk about the events of the day. There was nothing in particular they wanted to say except that they thought I had been treated unfairly. While sympathy seemed to be in short supply and I was delighted to receive even a little, I knew that more was at stake than merely my bruised feelings.

This was not a time to be sentimental. So I drew out the young people to learn of their feelings about race relations and what they thought ought to be done. They admitted that prejudice was present in this land and blamed their parents, more or less. Then we talked about why the black youth in the conference felt a need to emphasize their racial difference rather than their common humanity. The issue was translated into boy-girl terms so that the conclusion would have a major impact. I asked the young people if they had known some girls who were so insecure about their humanity that they felt the need always to relate to others in terms of their femininity. Most students admitted that they had known such persons. The principle was extended to the black youth. Maybe they felt a need to emphasize their race because they did not feel accepted as human beings, I suggested.

Then we talked about the responsibility of accepting. A few young people said they believed in meeting the other person halfway. Special circumstances of a relationship in love might require that one person go, not halfway, I reminded the young people, but all of the way to meet and reach another. Moreover, a special obligation was on the majority or the dominant people of power to over-extend themselves to the minority or the people with less power. I restated a principle that I had mentioned earlier in the conference that, from those unto whom much is given, more is required. Also, I talked about the need for whites to pursue blacks in a spirit of love and interde-pendence because, alone, whites stand incomplete. Such pursuit was a risky venture, however, and might result in some minor or major discomforts; but in the end it would be worth the effort.

Finally, I brought out that race and clan were of limited relevance in classifying individuals, that their humanity is what really matters. The outstanding task, as I saw it, was for the white youth to approach and accept the black youth as human beings so that the blacks could experience the irrelevance of race and not have to relate to others with race uppermost in their minds.

THE SIGN ON THE PIPE

Meanwhile some of the white youth were preparing another sign as our discussion about race continued. Around a pipe that extended through the basement and hung near the ceiling, they had wrapped several squares of paper and were printing a large letter on each square. I could see that it said something about a cookie. When finished, the simple message read

BROTHERHOOD IS AN OREO COOKIE

That message remained up throughout the night and until the end of the conference. It was an important idea to remember. These youth had turned a symbol of insult and alienation into one of support and reconciliation. Indeed the healing process began that night among the young as well as the old.

The last hour of the day was rapidly approaching. I still had work to do. Black youth were slowly wandering into the hall for the late-night snack of chili. The white youth were already there. I sensed that something dramatic might happen that night. I thought it best to be on my way. So I excused myself from the seminar session and went to my room to write.

Then a real confrontation took place. Screaming and crying, the black girl who had designed the original Oreo cookie banner shouted out.

"Why should I ever trust white people? They always hurt me, and you will too! That's why we don't have anything to do with you!"

"But I'm not just 'white people,' I'm me! I'm a person, and I don't want to hurt you!" one of the white boys answered her in a loud voice.

The confrontation was intense and went on as a shouting match for nearly half an hour. It was the last confrontation that the young people experienced. After that, they began to draw together to plan a service of Holy Communion for the entire conference for Thursday night. They were beginning to turn toward each other.

While the confrontation was taking place between black and white youth, adults were meeting in small interracial groups in dormitory rooms all over the campus, talking into the wee hours of the morning, trying to deal with the hostilities of that day and their anger that had been generated by the Manifesto, trying to explain their feelings of oppression, trying to find a plausible explanation, trying to capture a bit of understanding. Yes, the reconciling process had begun.

Thursday morning, the lecture was almost anticlimactic. Participants had found many of the answers themselves. My major function was to talk about the Manifesto and also to put the episode of the Oreo cookie in proper perspective. I mentioned how, in fewer than six hours, a symbol of separation and division had evolved into a symbol of integration and unity. I suggested that Hood Conference '69 might be remembered as the Conference of the Oreo Cookie. The cookie was symbolic of so much. It pointed toward the brokenness and estrangement in human society and the eternal possibility of reuniting.

THE YOUNG PEOPLE DO THEIR THING

The remainder of the day was uneventful. An attitude of anticipation prevailed, though, for all that was to come, for the known and unknown that had become a part of this conference.

After dinner and the evening lecture, the young people did their thing. The liturgy was new and different. There were strumming guitars and strange-sounding records. But most of all there was a warm embrace for all.

After Holy Communion, the youngsters flipped back to a fine Jewish expression—*Shalom*. For nearly thirty minutes, conference members wandered around the room kissing and embracing each other and shouting, *"Shalom!"* It was a happy, joyful occasion and a wonderful lift from a period of strife.

There were black and white people, men and women, northerners and southerners, the young and the old, hugging and kissing each other. Some may have thought it silly. But most people acted as if it were sacred to let loose and express their love for one another. Toward the end of the period of celebration, I sought out the designer of the first sign and placed a kiss upon her cheek. The original sign had disappeared. Only the brotherhood sign remained as the conference continued to unite.

A new topic was needed for the Friday morning lecture, not the one I had planned to present. I talked about repentance, redemption, and reconciliation. Also I dealt with the function of conflict.

"Members of most communities," I said, "yearn for a sweet and harmonious situation of peaceful cooperation. But often we cannot reach the stage of peaceful cooperation without first going through the turbulence of conflict or confrontation. It is well that we learn to endure it in love. This is the lesson that this conference has taught us."

A preacher from Pennsylvania summed up the conference this way: "By Friday at the closing Liturgy, the whole drama had been acted out, and the degree of reconciliation was beautiful. The black youth and the white youth were holding each other and laughing; they were together." He said that the message of hope and reconciliation had been acted out in a way that couldn't be put into words. The adult woman who had supported the angry black teenager embraced Mary Sue and me at the closing worship service, which was held out of doors on the campus. I was deeply moved by her expression of affection.

Oreo cookies were distributed. A man from Pennsylvania wanted to break bread together. He offered a piece of his Oreo cookie. I took it and ate it in grace.

"It was so beautiful," the preacher said. "It was so beautiful." I am persuaded to believe that it was.

CHAPTER 2

LIVING
IN, BETWEEN, AND BEYOND
THE RACES

History is full of examples of creative marginality, of people who have lived not only in but also between and beyond the races of humankind. When separateness is being endorsed by blacks as well as whites and integration as a national goal is under severe attack by liberals as well as conservatives, there is a need to interpret these actions. This book is one such attempt.

THE HIGH PRICE
WE'VE PAID FOR TRIBALISM

Given the present circumstances of American society and the racial tribal groups in which it is organized, integration in the near future does not seem to be an expected alterna-

24

tive. But neither is separatism a viable long-range option. This book describes the marginal people who live in, between, and beyond the races. It is they who are most likely to help our pluralistic society survive. The marginal people unite the clans and races in society and help us reconcile our differences.

We are ignoring the warnings of the past in our deliberate attempts to tribalize this nation and to frustrate the development of a genuine pluralistic community of interdependent people. When this nation was founded toward the close of the 18th century, its Constitutional Convention sanctioned slavery and racial discrimination. The first time this nation failed in human relationships, then, was at its beginning. It paid dearly for this failure after the middle of the 19th century with more than half a million lives lost in a civil war which was fought to end slavery, which could have been ended when the nation began.

Our nation did not learn from this tragic experience. At the close of the 19th century, the Supreme Court sanctioned racial segregation in its "separate but equal" doctrine. Again, we paid dearly for this miscarriage of justice. After the middle of the 20th century, our urban communities began to go up in smoke as a kind of civil war returned to the streets of our cities. The number of dead has been mounting ever since.

James B Conant, former President of Harvard, became the chief prophet for public education in the late 1950s and early 1960s. In his famous book *Slums and Suburbs,* Dr Conant [1961] said that, had integration in schools occurred one hundred years ago when blacks were first made free, a different situation would exist today. He said a caste system finds its clearest manifestation in an educational system.

On the basis of my research [Willie and Levy 1972] concerning black students at white colleges and their high school experiences following the Supreme Court decision in 1954 (which outlawed racial segregation in public education), I conclude that life is different for those who experience racial integration. Youth who experience integrated education are likely to have more interracial contacts in college than college students who were not educated in integrated high schools.

Racial reconciliation occurs among people who meet one another. Racial reconciliation is not so much an attitude as it is an action. The state of race relations in this country might have been different today, as suggested by Conant, had black and white children been educated together in the past. One black student at a predominantly white college analyzed his experience this way:

"If you don't try to bridge the gap," he said, "you just add to the troubles you already have—like prejudice, hate, and war." The words which this young man spoke were his own. But the wisdom they conveyed belongs to the ages.

In ancient times, there was Moses, a marginal man: Born as a Hebrew slave, reared as a wealthy Egyptian, and eventually married to an Ethiopian or black woman.* In modern times, there were Martin Buber and Martin Luther King, Jr, the new marginal men who lived in, between, and beyond their races. They, too, tried to reconcile the peoples of this world. They left a legacy of creative marginality.

If marginality is so creative, why do so few aspire to be marginal people? Why are race and clan relationships exalted?

Our hypothesis is that many people are fearful of marginality—are reluctant to live in, between, and beyond their race—because of their fear of loss of identity. They think they are maximizing their identity by relating primarily to like-minded and look-alike people when, in essence, they are limiting the range of their identity. Thus they can be looked upon as suffering a partial loss of identity, like the black teenager at the Hood Conference, discussed in Chapter 1.

John Gardner [1968, pp 145-146] describes identity as the assurance that comes from knowing and being known, and he calls the loss of identity a failure in the relationship between the individual and society. Gardner further states

*Numbers 12:1-3. The Cushites were from the land of Cush, identified as Ethiopia.

[p 148], "Those who suffer from a sense of anonymity [a loss of identity] would feel better if they could believe that their society needed them."

IDENTIFIED BY THE OTHERS

The search for identity thus seems to be a search for security and acceptance and a need to be needed by others. In the end, therefore, full identity depends upon one's actions as well as societal reactions, including the reactions of friends and enemies. Identity is a result of affirmation and confirmation, knowing and being known, needing and being needed. Identity involves personal action and group reaction.

This idea, of course, is different from the idea that identity can be found within oneself by drawing apart from the whole, by pulling apart from society at large. Identity, then, is a social process in which there is a negotiation between what a person thinks himself to be and what others believe him to be. The negotiating process is continuous, sometimes painful, sometimes pleasant. The anonymous people of this world, often referred to as invisible, are those who withdraw or who are pushed out of the social negotiating process. They suffer a loss of identity, either because they no longer affirm their personal significance or because others refuse to recognize their social worth.

The lives of the two Martins—Martin Buber and Martin Luther King, Jr—are adequate examples of how one finds a wide ranging identity and a sense of community by turning toward rather than away from the opposition and insisting on being recognized.

Martin Buber, for example, was a Zionist. Arthur Cohen [1957, p 29] states that Zionism for many Jews became "the cloak of pride, the instrument of masking their alienation and lack of roots in European soil." For Buber, however, Zionism was "the means of renewing roots, the ultimate device of reestablishing, not surrendering, contact with the European tradition."

Beyond his connection with Europe, in 1938, when Buber was forced to leave Germany and go to Israel, he in-

sisted that Israel ought to be a state of two nations in
which Arabs and Jews should jointly participate and share.
At one time he lived in the Arab sector of Israel. Moreover
he returned to Germany, amid much criticism, to receive
the Peace Prize of the German Book Trade [Cohen 1957,
p 35].

Martin Luther King, Jr, was one of the greatest leaders
this nation has ever experienced. His goal was total liberation for all people, his actual work being especially with
poor black people. He always tried to achieve a double
victory—one for the former oppressed and for the former
oppressors.

King saw the strength of black people as uniquely American. Yet he believed that there were similarities between
the black struggle and the struggle of the people of Israel
against the oppression of the ancient Pharaoh [1967, p
170]. He believed that black people ought to unite. Yet
he said [p 150]

> The future of the deep structural changes we seek will
> not be found in the decaying political machines. It lies
> in new alliances of Negroes, Puerto Ricans, labor, liber-
> als, certain church and middle-class elements.*

King was unhappy with the black power slogan because he
believed it divided society and, to him, meant black domi-
nation rather than black equality. Yet he engaged in direct
action in the public square as a powerful way of stating
the case of blacks.

He understood the origin of the black power slogan and
presented the most incisive analysis that I have seen. His
analysis is relevant to the discussion about identity [1967,
pp 32-33]:

> First, it is necessary to understand that Black Power is
> a cry of disappointment. The Black Power slogan did
> not spring full grown from the head of some philosophi-
> cal Zeus. It was born from the wounds of despair and
> disappointment. It is a cry of daily hurt and persistent

pain.   For centuries the Negro has been caught in the tentacles of white power.   Many Negroes have given up faith in the white majority because "white power" with total control has left them empty-handed.   So in reality the call for Black Power is a reaction to the failure of white power.*

He further stated, "Anyone familiar with the Black Power movement recognizes that defiance of white authority and white power is a constant theme; the defiance almost becomes a kind of taunt" [1967, p 40].*

Thus the call for black power, according to the King analysis, is but another example of a failure in relationship between the black individual and white society.   Society has failed to make it clear that it needs black people.   Accordingly black people have begun to assert themselves in desperation to obtain the attention they need for survival.   Riots are an irrational way of raging at a society that has neglected the oppressed.

Were there no challenges to the personal significance or the social survival of black people by white people, there would be no need to call for black power, no need to riot and rage.

THE MORE A GROUP IS THREATENED, THE MORE IT RETREATS

When group survival is threatened, then group identity is emphasized.   Robert Park recognized this fact in the Introduction which he wrote for Everett Stonequist's book entitled *The Marginal Man.*   Park [1937, p xiii] said, "The loyalties that bind together the members of . . . the clan and the tribe . . . are in direct proportion to the intensity of the fears and hatreds with which they view their enemies and rivals in the larger intertribal . . . world."   But no group, black or white, can confirm its own identity.   A group, like a person, may engage in self-affirmation but must be confirmed by another.

Speaking of individuals, Martin Buber said that the "essence of man . . . can be directly known only in a living relationship. Or the *I* . . . exists only through the relationship to the *Thou*" [Buber 1957, p 205]. Applying this principle to the races, one might assert that *blacks exist and are significant as a people, in part, through their relationship with whites;* conversely, *whites exist and are significant as a people, in part, through their relationship with blacks.*

When blacks or whites attempt to find meaning, security, and significance (which may be translated as identity) within themselves, they usually attempt this because the total society is not giving them a feeling of meaning, security, and significance. Other groups are not confirming the identity of the group that is trying to confirm its own identity. Self-confirmation, like self-love, is an action of doubtful value, arising from desperation. A group never can be really certain of its social significance in the scheme of things if only the members of that group believe it is valuable. A group rejected, ignored, or unrecognized tends to be uncertain of itself.

The two-stage process of identity—affirmation and confirmation—is necessary at all levels of society. It is necessary in the family and kinship or clan structure. Most people, black and white, are confirmed in their personhood in these structures. It is necessary also in the society at large.

The peoplehood status of whites tends to be confirmed by the society at large. But the way of life of blacks, their various organizations and associations, are often ignored. Confirmation for personhood status at the family, kinship, or clan level is no substitute for confirmation of peoplehood status by the society at large.

James Coleman indicates how integrated education contributes to this confirmation at the society level. He said, "Negro children in an integrated school come to gain a greater sense of their efficacy to control their destiny. It is very likely due to the fact that they see that they can do some things better than whites and can perform in school better than some whites, a knowledge which they never had so long as they were isolated in an all-black school" [Coleman 1968, p 25].

Melvin Tumin [1969, pp 20–21] has said that the chances for acceptance are much greater when the outsiders have achieved powerful and prestigious social and economic positions. This is what is meant by the statement that "green money turns black people white." This, of course, is the error in most analyses of racial identity. They are based on a simplistic black-and-white analysis which assumes that all identity problems would be resolved if blacks would learn to think and act like whites. It is interesting to note that the statement is seldom reversed. It would appear to be unthinkable to say that whites could solve their identity problem by attempting to think and act like blacks. Yet this too must be considered as a possibility.

CONFIRMING OUR VALUE AS PERSONS

Whites need confirmation of their personhood, just as do blacks. Almost automatically blacks have, in the past, confirmed the personhood of the whites. Blacks have always given confirmation, sometimes willingly sometimes grudgingly. Even when blacks speak disparagingly of a white, they may call him "the man"—a term which denotes humanity. But whites, speaking disparagingly of blacks, refer to them as "coons" and "jungle bunnies," and other non-human animals. Whites have not so willingly confirmed the personhood of blacks. In fact, whites have been advised to practice "benign neglect" with reference to blacks. Hence, the preoccupation of blacks with their identity.

Indeed, one might conjecture that the separatist movement among blacks as manifested in the convening of a black caucus is threatening to some whites because it is a sign that blacks may take the next step and withhold or deny personhood confirmation for whites as whites did in their segregated groups in earlier years. Many whites, however, endorse the black separatist movement because of their misunderstanding of their need for blacks. As stated above, because blacks have always confirmed the personhood of whites, many whites have never raised the question of what would happen to them if they were neglected by blacks. It is beyond the comprehension of many whites that they could be rejected by blacks, with harmful consequences.

THE NEW CONCEPT OF
MARGINAL MAN

An early concept of marginal man was that of one who falls between two social or cultural groups [Stonequist 1937, p 2]. The new concept of the marginal person, as I see it, is one who rises above two social or cultural groups, freeing the different groups to work together. Martin Buber and Martin Luther King, Jr, were the latter kind of marginal men. Of Martin Luther King, Jr, writer William Robert Miller [1968, p 292] said, "In the end he was misunderstood . . . by both white liberals and black militants. . . ." At the time of King's death, Stokely Carmichael, the modern reviver of the idea of black power who challenged the leadership of King during the Mississippi March, said:

> When white America killed Dr. King . . . she lost it. . . . He was the one man in our race who was trying to teach our people to have love, compassion and mercy for white people.

Also, it must be said that King was trying to teach white people to have love, compassion, and mercy for black people. This is why we call him the new marginal man, one who found his identity neither among blacks nor among whites, but in the synthesis of these two races. Park conceived of the marginal man as one whom fate had condemned to live in two worlds. The new concept of the marginal man is one to whom fate has given the opportunity to unite two different worlds because he lives in, between, and beyond his social or cultural groups.

CHAPTER 3

RACISM, VIOLENCE, AND INSTITUTIONAL NORMS

The expressions of racism which often are outcomes of the practice of segregation and separatism are a confirmation for mutual destruction. The Prologue to Ralph Ellison's prize-winning book, *The Invisible Man,* demonstrates this. Ponder his report of racial hostility and hate and the near murder that black and white racism engendered.

One night I accidentally bumped into a man, and perhaps because of the near darkness he saw me and called me an insulting name. I sprang at him, seized his coat lapels and demanded that he apologize. He was a tall blond man, and as my face came close to his he looked insolently out of his blue eyes and cursed me, his breath hot in my face as he struggled. I pulled his chin down sharp upon the crown of my head, butting him as I had seen the West Indians do, and I felt his flesh tear and the blood gush out, and I yelled, "Apologize! Apologize!" But he continued to curse and struggle, and I butted him again and again until he went down heavily, on his knees, profusely bleeding. I kicked him repeatedly, in a frenzy because he still uttered insults though his lips were frothy with blood. Oh yes, I kicked him! And in my outrage I got out my knife and prepared to slit his throat, right there beneath the lamplight in the deserted street, holding him by the collar with one hand, and opening the knife with my teeth—when it occurred to me that the man had not seen me, actually; that he, as far as he knew, was in the midst of a walking nightmare! And I stopped the blade, slicing the air as I pushed him away, letting him fall back to the street. I stared at him hard as the lights of a car stabbed through the darkness. He lay there, moaning on the asphalt; a man almost killed by a phantom. It unnerved me. I was both disgusted and ashamed. I was like a drunken man myself, wavering about on weakened legs. Then I was amused. Something in this man's thick head had sprung out and beaten him within an inch of his life. I began to laugh at this crazy discovery. Would he have awakened at the point of death? Would Death himself have freed him for wakeful living? But I didn't linger. I ran away into the dark, laughing so hard I feared I might rupture myself. The next day I saw his picture in the *Daily News,* beneath a caption stating that he had been "mugged." Poor fool, poor, blind fool, I thought with sincere compassion, mugged by an invisible man! [Ellison 1952, p 8] *

The question is: Who was responsible for this near murder—the man who was beaten or the man who did the beating? Another question: Who could have brought an end to the hostilities? Finally: What was the role of racism?

Jacques Barzun answers the last question this way: Racism "utters a blind commandment to shed blood" [1965, p xix]. The commandment was dutifully obeyed as a black and a white man interacted in a deadly dance which anthropologist Stanley Diamond has called "a hellish minuet" [1965, p 474].

Charles Silberman wrote a series of articles on race for *Fortune* magazine in the early 1960s. In his book *Crisis in Black and White* (which was an elaboration of these articles), he called the blacks in America "the key to our mutual future" [1964, p 15]. Racism is not a phenomenon which visits oppression upon the disadvantaged only. Racism could result in the death and destruction of all.

DESTINED TO LEAD ALL OTHERS

Racism is based on the belief that one's own people, because of their unique qualities and characteristics, are the source and center of creation and are destined to lead all others, who are inferior and incapable of leading themselves. Werner Stark's [1966] book *The Sociology of Religion* is filled with illustrations of racism: the "sacred" nation, under the "sacred" ruler, carrying out its "sacred" mission, which often ends in bloodshed. A poem by Thich Nhat Han, the Vietnamese Buddhist monk, asks the rhetorical question: "Who will be left to celebrate the victory made of blood and fire?"

The increasing urbanization of this nation is bringing all sorts and conditions of people into each other's presence in the city. Racism makes it impossible for people who need each other to be near each other. No nation can set its people against each other and remain strong.

Charles Silberman attempts to identify one way in which society pays for this transgression. He writes, "Man cannot deny the humanity of his fellow man without ultimately destroying his own" [Silberman 1964, p 16].

Hylan Lewis, a sociologist, has recorded an illustration of racism expressed by a white foreman in the Washington, D C, metropolitan area in the middle of the 1960s.

Interviewer: Do you have any blacks working under you?

Foreman: No. Right now we are building a house for

an army colonel. We never use blacks on jobs in Maryland and Virginia because that would hurt the company's reputation.

Interviewer: Do you ever use blacks?

Foreman: When we have a job in Washington, we hire a large number of blacks.

Interviewer: Why?

Foreman: The white painter gets $28 a day. The black is able and willing to do the same job for only $14. Give me a crew of six niggers and we'll knock out a five-story office building in a week. They all got families, and $14 a day is damn good money for a nigger [Willie 1969b, p 11].

Charles Silberman has recorded an illustration of racism expressed by a Black Muslim minister in California in the early 1960s.

On Sunday June 3, 1962, when news was flashed around the United States that a chartered airplane bound from Paris to Atlanta had crashed, killing 130 of the people aboard, Malcolm X, then the number two man in the Black Muslim movement, . . . was delivering a sermon to fifteen hundred Muslims in Los Angeles. He immediately shared the good news with his audience: I would like to announce a very beautiful thing that has happened. . . . Somebody came and told me that [God] had answered our prayers in France. He dropped an airplane out of the sky with over 120 white people in it because the Muslims believe in an eye for an eye and a tooth for a tooth. But thanks to God, or Jehovah, or Allah, we will continue to pray and we hope that every day another plane falls out of the sky. . . . We call on our God—He gets rid of 120 of them at one whop [Silberman 1964, pp 55-56].*

Although Malcolm X, a gifted man, later overcame such a short-sighted perspective, it is important to realize the hatred that he had at that time. Then there is the story that is told in jest by whites:

A black man at his death approached the Pearly Gates of Heaven, where St Peter welcomed him. After being sure that the black was comfortable, St Peter asked him, "Have you ever done anything in your life that would make the Lord happy?"

"Well, St Peter, you see I'm just an unimportant man. I've never done anything important."

"Surely, man, you must have done something to make glad the heart of the Lord," replied St Peter.

"Well, of course, I did work for integration," said the black. "I was the first black man to marry a white woman in Tupelo, Mississippi."

"That's wonderful," replied St Peter. "That's just the kind of thing that will make the Lord happy. When did this happen?"

"This morning," said the black.

Another version of the same story in the folklore of whites is about a black who was asked by St Peter what he had done to make the Lord happy.

"Why I integrated the White Baptist Church in the town where I lived down on earth."

"That's the kind of thing that will make the Lord very happy," replied St Peter.

"Yes," replied the black, "But there's one thing that I evidently didn't understand. I thought when they baptized you that they let you up out of the water again."

Such expressions of racism are what have been called by Silberman "animal-like hatred." And so they are. So is it all—the hate of the white foreman for blacks and the hate of the black minister for whites and the hate of people who joke about racial murders. Note the disdain for the sanctity of human life in the joke about God and the plane crash of whites or the cavalier attitude about human death in the joke about God and the murder of blacks. Silberman [1964, p 56] makes this observation: "There's no reason to assume that black men are more immune to the cancer of hate than white men." Indeed, blacks and whites are engaged in a hellish minuet that can be only a dance unto death if appropriate interventions are not made.

PUBLIC APPROVAL
OF RACISM

To overcome racism, we must have deliberate institutional change. Abraham Kardiner and Lionel Ovesey [1962, p 380], two psychiatrists, have stated that it is quixotic to attempt to educate an individual out of a stereotyped prejudice while there is continuing public approval for the prejudice.

Racism may be based on prejudice. That is an attitude that we take toward others. Racism itself is an open act of oppression. Gordon Allport said [1958, pp 459–460], "Theoretically, perhaps the best of all methods for changing attitudes is under conditions of individual psychotherapy, for . . . prejudice is often deeply embedded in the functioning of the entire personality." However, Allport follows this theoretical statement with a cautionary note, pointing out that "the frequency of transformation under therapeutic . . . conditions is unknown" and that, from a practical point of view, the proportion of the population that can be reached with psychotherapy will always be small. Allport is more certain about the effects of law, which might be classified as a form of institutional intervention. He states that "legislation . . . becomes educative" and that "laws . . . act as a restraint." By and large, "laws will be obeyed," Allport said [1958, pp 440, 442], "if they are in line with one's conscience."

One problem in approaching racism, therefore, is how to make a breakthrough in the conscience of America. It is a known fact that some of the signers of the Declaration of Independence were owners of slaves and that President Abraham Lincoln insisted that "reunion was the only aim [of the Civil War] even after he had drafted a proclamation to emancipate the slaves" [Handlin 1963, p 256]. America has a long history of failing to face up to racism and its weakening effects.

This is our condition in America today. There needs to be a basic change in the institutions of our society and in our ways of living together if we are to move this society toward a helpful situation in which the races can each contribute to the enrichment of all humankind.

Racism is the overt act of limiting the opportunities of persons in specific racial groups. The reason for calling for institutional change as a way of curbing racism is because of new information provided by Thomas Pettigrew. He found that approximately "three-fifths [of white Americans] are prejudiced for largely conformity reasons." He feels that this finding "casts serious doubt upon the appropriateness . . . of the traditional case-by-case medical model for remedial action." He concludes that what is needed is "a structural model for remedial action . . . that places greatest importance as a target for change . . . on the racist institutional structures that shape and support the bigotry of individuals." He states that "the conformers go right on conforming" and that institutional change for the purpose of establishing nonracist norms "would set a new reference and new expectations for conformers to live up to" [Pettigrew 1973, pp 293-294]. In the next chapter we will discuss the kinds of people most likely to initiate needed institutional change.

CHAPTER 4

MARGINALITY
AND SOCIAL CHANGE

This is a period when all around us we hear the call for unity as a way of building an effective power base to foster or withstand social change. Our hypothesis in this chapter is that unity is not enough, that marginality as described in Chapter 2 is an essential component in a healthy human society. Moreover, we assert that effective social systems endure the tension between the need for unity and the requirement for marginality. We know a great deal about unity and stability but not so much about marginality and social change.

The marginal man, according to Stonequist, "is poised in psychological uncertainty between two (or more) social worlds" [Stonequist 1937, pp 6-8]. In general, Stonequist discussed marginality as a negative effect.

RELATIVELY
THE MORE CIVILIZED

Only in the last chapter of his book did Stonequist recognize in a limited way any positive contribution of marginality in human society. In a very brief discussion, he pointed out that "the marginal man is the key-personality in the contacts of cultures. It is in his mind that the cultures come together, conflict, and eventually work out some kind of mutual adjustment and interpretation." Stonequist concluded that "the life histories of marginal men offer the most significant material for the analysis of the cultural process as it springs from the contact of social groups" [Stonequist 1937, p 222].

Robert Park, who was Stonequist's teacher, saw the marginal person not so much as a supersensitive and uncertain individual. Rather he considered the marginal person to be "the individual with the wider horizon, the keener intelligence, the more detached and rational viewpoint." In fact he said, "The marginal man is always relatively the more civilized human being." According to Park, the marginal person—the more civilized human being—"occupies the position which has been historically that of the Jew in the Diaspora" [Park 1937, p xviii] and, I might add, that of blacks and other racial minorities in America. Of course, it may be difficult for persons who have not controlled their ethnocentrism to call Jews, blacks, and other minorities more civilized. But that is what Robert Park said of Jews. I believe that he shared a significant insight in that statement and that he indicated an understanding of the function of marginality that is similar to the discussion in Chapter 2.

Harvey Cox, in his book *The Secular City,* made a comment similar to that of Park. He said, "[the Jews], when they were wandering and homeless . . . seem to have been closest to fulfilling their calling" [Cox 1965, p 55]. Cox probably achieved this insight because his analysis of urban society focused more upon freedom and social process than upon control and social structure. In fact he indicates in the subtitle that his book is a celebration of the liberties of the secular city and is an invitation to its discipline. Most sociological studies begin first with an analysis of patterns of discipline or social control and eventually may get around to analyzing alternative expressions of freedom and social change. But many sociological studies never get this far.

In the 1960s during the height of the civil rights revolution, Commissioner James Allen of the Department of Education in New York State, was asked what, in his opinion, had made the greatest contribution to change in the educational system in that state. He seriously considered the question for a while and then responded that blacks in their demonstrations, in their peaceful demonstrations, had probably done more than any other group to bring about educational change, and he urged them to continue their efforts. Apparently the peaceful demonstrations benefited all parts of society. Please note that Commissioner Allen did not refer to the powerful Board of Regents in New York State as the primary initiator of educational change. It seems that Allen was trying to tell us something about the role of marginal people in social change.

It is interesting to note that the blacks who have been recommended for receipt of the Nobel Prize for Peace have been residents of the United States and the Union of South Africa, two countries in which they are subdominant or marginal people in terms of political power. Apparently their experiences as marginals have contributed to their leadership capacity to seek peace.

IF BLACKS WOULD ACT
LIKE WHITES

A proper understanding of the function of marginality in human society would have prevented Daniel Patrick Moynihan from prescribing that blacks be made over in the image of whites in his 1965 report on the black family. Specifically, Moynihan said that retardation of the progress of blacks as a group is due to the fact that their alleged matriarchal family structure is *"so out of line* with the rest of American society" [US Dept of Labor 1965, p 29] (italics added). The implication is clear that, if blacks would act like whites in their family life, they might be treated like whites. According to this formulation, blacks are responsible for their own oppression, especially those blacks in female-headed, one-parent families. Arthur Jensen in 1969 made a similar case with reference to intelligence. He stated that "The remedy deemed logical for children who would do poorly in school is to boost their IQ's up to where they can perform *like the majority . . ."* [Jensen 1969, p 3] (italics added). Again the implication is clear: If blacks would think like whites, they might be treated like whites. Neither Moynihan nor Jensen remotely considered that what blacks do and think may be what they ought to do and think in terms of their existential condition and that what they do and think might ultimately be beneficial for whites too. One can understand this principle if one can understand the function of marginality in social life.

For example, the employment of black women outside the home as workers in the national labor force was a pioneering marginal activity over the years which eventually resulted in an increasing number of white women being employed outside the home. Had blacks been made over in the image of whites as prescribed by some social scientists, white women would not have been able to observe the creative effects of work for pay as they were able to do by observing the work experience of black women. Back in 1940 only 25% of the mature white women 35 to 44 years of age were in the labor force compared with 45% of the black women. Today about half of the mature white women are in the labor force compared with about 60% of the black women [US Bureau of Census 1972, pp 1-372]. Thus the gap between the proportion of women in the labor force in the two racial populations is narrowing.

Joe Feagin has reported that, as far back as 1900, about 4 out of every 10 black women were members of the labor force, a proportion far greater than that for whites [Feagin 1970, p 23]. The opportunity to work has been a creative experience for black women over the years, possibly related to "rising family aspirations for a higher standard of living . . ." [Feagin 1970, p 24]. White working women probably are unaware of the fact that they may be modeling their behavior after blacks.

The enlarged proportion of black women in the labor force compared with whites repeatedly has been referred to as an overrepresentation of black women. The phrase "overrepresentation" can be used only if the labor force participation rate for white women is looked upon as the norm for all women. It is interesting to note that seldom are white women said to be underrepresented in the labor force compared with blacks. This statement is seldom made because most social analysts do not hold up the behavior of blacks or other minorities as an archetype or model for whites or the majority. Yet, if it is appropriate to say that black women have been overrepresented in the labor force, it is appropriate to say that white women have been underrepresented. Most social analysts are inclined to make the first statement because they have not adequately recognized that their attitudes are ethnocentric, that they use happenings within their own group as a criterion of what ought to be. They still believe that the way of life of the majority should be the model for the minority. This attitude has been clearly spelled out by Moynihan and Jensen.

When the majority has an ethnocentric view of social organization, it fails to recognize the unique and significant contributions of marginal people whatever their age, sex, race, or social class may be; moreover, we fail to recognize that the adaptations of the subdominant, minority, or marginal group may be beneficial for all, including the majority and the minority.

THE REBEL AND SOCIETY

As black women demonstrated to white women the benefits of employment in the labor force, marginal people in general have led the way and pointed to a new day. We are not alone in making this observation. Robert Merton has stated, "It is not infrequently the case that the non-conforming minority in a society represents the interest and ultimate values of the group more effectively than the conforming majority" [Merton 1949, p 367]. I like the way René Dubos has stated the case for marginality. He calls the rebel "the standard-bearer of the visionaries who gradually increase man's ethical stature." Also he believes that "as long as there are rebels in our midst, there is reason to hope that our societies can be saved" [Dubos 1968, pp 5–6]. For those who have given their primary allegiance to the study of social structure, social control, and *homeostasis,* the Dubos statement may appear to be sentimentalism. But for those who recognize the need to study social process as well as social structure, or *homeokinesis* as well as *homeostasis,* this statement points in the direction of that which has been neglected in our sociological research.

HOMEOSTASIS
AND HOMEOKINESIS

As those who are familiar with physiology well know, the concept *homeostasis*—a theoretical formulation of the tendency for organic systems to maintain a steady state, constantly correcting for imbalance and disequilibrium—was introduced by the Harvard physiologist Walter B Cannon [1939]. It was readily adopted by social scientists such as Talcott Parsons and others and became a major frame of reference for organizing our thoughts about social organization as well as organic systems.

Homeostasis, a basic concept which aids us to organize our thoughts about living systems, was not challenged until the recent writings of the Rockefeller University microbiologist René Dubos. Categorically, he has stated, "Living systems are characterized not by homeostasis, but by homeokinesis" [Dubos 1972, p 249]. With reference to physiology, Dubos states, "Homeostatic processes that appear to be successful because they exert protective or reparative function at the time they occur commonly elicit malfunction at a later date." For example, "The production of scar tissue is a homeostatic response because it heals wounds and helps in checking the spread of infection. But in the liver or the kidney, scar tissue means cirrhosis or glomerular nephritis; in rheumatoid arthritis, it may freeze the joints; and in the lung it may choke the breathing process." Dubos concluded, "When the end results of homeostasis are evaluated over a long period of time, it becomes obvious that the wisdom of the body is often a short-sighted wisdom" [Dubos 1972, p 248]. Dubos then went on to state why homeostasis—the tendency for living systems to maintain a steady state—is not an appropriate concept for the purpose of analyzing social systems. "Man differs from the rest of the animal kingdom," said Dubos, "not by his biological endowments but by the use he has made of them, usually in a conscious way." He called our attention to the fact that man is reflective and interpretive: man thinks and reflects about what he sees, and he interprets it, trying to find meaning in what he encounters. Dubos was critical of social scientists who have adopted the homeostatic attitude toward man. He stated that this causes such scientists to be "insensitive to the potentialities for social change." In fact he states, "The concept of homeostasis in sociology and economics, like the concept of climax in ecology, is a postulate which hardly ever fits reality" [Dubos 1972, pp 248-49]. Indeed living systems must maintain a continuous rate of change, or homeokinesis; otherwise they atrophy, decay, or disintegrate.

As we see it, homeokinesis is not so much a concept in opposition to homeostasis as it is complementary to it. In social groups, we have both the tendency to maintain our traditions and customs and another tendency to transcend, change, and reach out beyond our present circumstances, what Dubos calls homeokinesis.

TRANSCENDENCE

A problem in contemporary as well as historical social science is the absence of a sense of transcendence—the ability to go beyond one's boundaries or limitations. Transcendence is what marginal people tend to bring to social organization. For example, in sociology the idea of the self is usually discussed as if each person tends to act in accordance with his or her understanding of the way others expect. This is part of the truth. This idea of the self focuses upon control, conformity, social expectation, and homeostasis. But people are not entirely passive agents who are acted upon by external forces.

Human beings are concerned with aesthetics too, with the beautiful. According to Lionel Trilling, it was Hegel who gave art an importance that it had never before had in moral philosophy. Hegel saw art as "the activity of man in which spirit expresses itself not only as utility, not only according to law, but as grace, as transcendence, as manner and style" [Trilling 1955, p xii]. To gain a proper understanding of the self and human society, we must consider the urge for freedom and change in people as well as the need for control and stability, the desire to try new things as well as to conform to the old, the tendency to homeokinesis as well as to homeostasis.

MOSES AND
MARTIN LUTHER KING, JR

Two classic social movements illustrate the function of marginal people as contributors to social change through the impact of their movements upon the total society. The ancient and contemporary freedom movements among Jews and blacks are quite similar and so are Moses and Martin Luther King, Jr, the people who led them. We present a brief analysis of these men as living examples of marginality and the kind of leadership that flows therefrom.

Earlier we said that social analysts such as Moynihan and Jensen have urged the minority to think and act like the majority as a way of overcoming oppression. When blacks have exhibited capacities so as to effectively compete with whites in America, they have been roundly put down by whites, and also they are dubbed as oreos by blacks. We would suppose that more people have read the autobiography of Malcolm X than the life story of Martin Luther King, Jr. Both, of course, were great men. But Martin Luther King, Jr, was university educated and comparatively well to do. Malcolm X was street educated and poor. Malcolm X could be idolized but looked down upon by middle-class persons who, therefore, found him to be a more acceptable folk hero. As mentioned in Chapter 2, Martin Luther King, Jr, was misunderstood by both white liberals and black militants [Miller 1968, p 294]. Even liberal social scientists and radical students have been quick to call educated blacks "white Negroes" and intelligent women "masculine." The stories of Martin and Moses should correct such ethnocentric tendencies.

The leaders of social movements need not necessarily possess the characteristics of the people whom they lead. Take Moses, for example. Moses was a marginal man all right. He had experiences very much unlike the enslaved Jewish people whom he led to freedom. Yet Moses was a magnificent leader whom the people followed for forty years.

Martin Luther King, Jr, "was born without fanfare in comfortable, . . . conventional circumstances" [Bennett 1964, p 5]. King's mother and father attended college. His father was the pastor of a leading Baptist church in Atlanta, Georgia. King earned academic degrees from Morehouse College, Crozer Theological Seminary, and Boston University. Lerone Bennett, King's schoolmate, described King's youth as "healthy, vital, [and] fun-loving" [Bennett 1964, p 17]. His family was definitely middle class. Yet Martin lost his life in Memphis where he came to participate in a demonstration with garbage workers. He too was a marginal man and a magnificent leader much unlike the poor people who followed him.

There were other similarities between these two men. Both had detractors among their own people who questioned their integrity and authenticity before and after their death. Sigmund Freud, the Jewish psychoanalyst, claimed that Moses actually was an Egyptian who tried to force his own monotheistic brand of religion upon Jewish people [Freud 1939, pp 3-65]. John A Williams, the black writer, claimed that Martin was a middle-class snob [Williams 1970, pp 151-154] who tried to force his own philosophy of nonviolent resistance upon black people [Williams 1970, p 57].

Both were leaders who demanded no dominion for themselves [Buber 1958, p 87]. Because of the immense power which Moses and Martin possessed despite the absence of any formal authority and because of their great humility, the two men often were puzzlements to their own people, as well as to others. From time to time they were murmured against, but the people continued to follow them. Moses and Martin had to contend with high governmental authorities who tried to restrict their movements, but they negotiated successfully in behalf of the enslaved and the poor

Martin Buber has an interesting observation on the marginal status of leaders of freedom movements. He has stated that one who is to be the liberator "has to be introduced into the stronghold of the alien." Freedom movements are "a kind of liberation which cannot be brought about by anyone who grew up as a slave, nor yet by anyone who is not connected with the slaves; but only by one of the latter who has been brought up in the midst of the aliens and has received an education equipping him with all their wisdom and powers . . ." [Buber 1958, p 35]. Moses was a liberator of slaves who was reared in the household of aristocrats. Martin was a liberator of the poor who was educated in the schools of the well-to-do. They did not grow up as slaves or as poor people but nevertheless were connected with them. They truly were marginal men who found identity in the synthesis of groups so that each person in the groups (and each group) could learn from the other and be more than what either was alone.

This concept of the marginal person as synthesizer recognizes that members of the out-group do not have to behave as if they were members of the in-group and that members of the minority do not have to think and act like members of the majority to be effective participants in society.

In conclusion, may we return to the Parkian idea that marginals are always a little more civilized than the rest of us. Is there anyone for marginality? Or are we all too busy unifying our separate tribes in a vain hope that that will bring self-confirmation?

CHAPTER 5

THE SIGNIFICANT
SOCIAL HISTORY OF BLACKS

Back in 1941, Richard Wright, a gifted black author, published a book, *12 Million Black Voices,* which was subtitled *A Folk History of the Negro in the United States.* Toward the end of that book, he discusses the black history that really matters. One can determine from this summary that black history in the New World has been characterized by courage, endurance, and transcendence:

> We look back over the road we have travelled and compare it with the road over which the white folk have travelled, and we see that three hundred years in the history of our lives are equivalent to two thousand years in the lives of the whites.
> During the three hundred years we have been in the new world, we have experienced all the various types of family life, all the many adjustments to rural and urban life, and today, weary but still eager, we stand

ready to accept more change. Imagine European history from the days of Christ to the present telescoped into three hundred years and you can comprehend the drama which our consciousness has experienced. Brutal, bloody, crowded with suffering abrupt transitions, the lives of us black folk represent the most magical and meaningful picture of human experience in the Western World.

Hurled from our native African homes into the very center of the most complex and highly industrialized civilization the world has ever known, we stand today with the consciousness and memory such as few people possess. We black folk, our history and our present being, are a mirror of all the manifold experiences of America. What we want, what we represent, what we endure is what America *is*. If we black folk perish, America will perish. If America has forgotten her past, then let her look into the mirror of our consciousness and she will see the *living* past living in the present, for our memories go back, through our black folk of today, through the recollection of our black parents, and through the tales of slavery told by our black grandparents, to the time when none of us, black or white, lived in this fertile land. . . .

Look at us and know us and you will know yourselves, for *we* are *you* looking back at you from the dark mirror of our lives [Wright and Rosskan 1941, pp 145-146].*

This is a powerful literary statement of human interdependence. A few phrases let me restate and emphasize. Richard Wright sensed the miracle of the 20th century, which is the life of the black people in America. He said, ". . . black folk represent the most magical and meaningful picture of human experience in the Western World." He also characterized black people as a "dark mirror." Then he commanded white people to look at blacks. By doing this, whites might begin to know themselves. According to Wright, this is the only way that whites in America may come to know themselves. White America cannot find its destiny apart from the destiny of black America. This is another way of saying what was said in Chapter 2, that the peoplehood of whites is, in part, a function of being confirmed by blacks.

THE CREATIVE DISSENTERS

The history of the black people in America which is significant, unique, and different, then, is not their contribution to art and science but their contribution to the process of humanizing America. This responsibility has fallen uniquely upon blacks because they are the population that this nation, when it was founded, tried to dehumanize and treat as property. It seems to be a law of life that the victims of oppression will continue to be victimized until they personally insist that the oppression cease.

Wright said that, if black people perish, America will perish. Martin Luther King, Jr, echoed a similar assertion in his last book. He pointed out that we are a nation of many peoples and that each group is dependent on the others, whether they wish to be or not. In such a huge nation where all are interdependent, no racial or ethnic group can retreat to itself [King 1967, p 61]. We are not islands sufficient unto ourselves, as John Donne said in his poem.

By calling attention to the interdependence of all racial and ethnic groups in America, King was reminding blacks that they must not become self-centered in their historical quest for liberation. Blacks and any other oppressed group cannot win their freedom at another's expense. In the process of upgrading their own economic status, King urged blacks, at the same time, to work for the uplift of other racial minorities such as Puerto Ricans, Chicanos, and Native Americans. Also he called attention to the poverty-stricken whites in Appalachia and said that blacks must be concerned about their economic plight. As he saw it, a meaningful war against poverty had to include all who were disadvantaged.

King felt that segregated schools in America, by and large, were inadequate. But his call for integration was twofold. He wanted racial integration along with improved education for all, blacks as well as whites. Referring to several nationwide studies of the quality of education in America, King said that some public school systems are using century-old methods that are inappropriate for the needs of children today [King 1967, pp 132–133].

The strength of the civil rights movement has been its inclusiveness. It has attacked inconsistencies between principles which have resulted in court rulings beneficial to all. Moreover, the civil rights movement has drawn upon the time and talent of people affiliated with many different interest groups. In this respect, the freedom movement for blacks has been a freedom movement for the nation.

Although black history is in part American history, the civil rights leaders insist that there are significant differences. A common theme has been that of creative dissent brilliantly articulated by Martin Luther King, Jr. This notion suggests that blacks and other minorities should not strive to become an integrated part of a defective society, but should participate for the purpose of reform. Effective participation by all should result in a new system of values for the whole nation. These values would stress fair and humane treatment of all people.

King felt that the history of black people in America had equipped them in a superb way to help the nation to develop a new system of values. The pain and suffering which blacks had experienced during their centuries of existence in slavery and semislavery had taught them that a nation without a soul of love and justice could be brutal despite its material wealth. This learning which had been deeply etched in the lives of blacks because of their "have-not status" should be shared with the entire nation.

King believed this to be a special calling of blacks—to confront the nation with its need to change. For what happened to blacks in the New World and Jews in the Old World could happen to any people, including those who now are the dominant people of power. A value system which sanctions the oppression of any people eventually could sanction the oppression of all people [King 1967, p 134].

Black people, therefore, have had a double history of freeing themselves from oppression and freeing the nation from the need to oppress. King called upon blacks to bear this burden of a unique history. If they would do this, he said, they would "inject new meaning into the veins of American life" and history would call them great [King 1967, p 134].

This orientation which guided and governed the freedom movement among blacks is significant history not only for blacks but also for whites. It is a history not of violence and bloody victories but of sacrifice and suffering for the redemption of a nation and its people, including the oppressors and the oppressed. Few, if any, freedom movements in the past have been as deeply concerned about the welfare of the opposition as well as about the welfare of those who are fighting the battle.

BLACKS—THE MIRROR FOR WHITES

Whites seldom understand how indebted they are to black people. That black people are the mirror of white people in America is comprehended in only a limited way by blacks as well as by whites. A proper understanding of the social history of black people in the United States might have stalled the segregationist movement among whites in the past and the separatist movement among blacks in the present. A proper understanding of the social history of black people might yet lead to reconciliation of a nation now divided.

Black people in the New World have a role and responsibility similar to those of Jewish people in the Old World as mentioned by Park in Chapter 3 of this book. They are called to reconcile the races of humankind. They are called to be the new marginal people. Thus the fight for the freedom of blacks in America, at the same time, is a fight for the liberation of whites in America, a liberation from fear and from the nearsightedness that comes from seeing only one point of view.

This is the meaning of the double victory of which Martin Luther King, Jr, often spoke. Whites are imprisoned by their compulsion to always be in charge. Blacks can liberate whites from this compulsion by refusing to be dealt with as if they were property and by assuming greater responsibility in the management of this nation and its communities, organizations, and associations. This way, black history and American history will be one.

This concept of black marginal people as synthesizers has an important characteristic: It does not require one to act as if he were a member of another group. Rather, the ways of each group are important, for they are used in putting together the new life—in the synthesis of the new life—in which each group can live more abundantly than before. In race, the new marginal persons are those who synthesize the ways of life of the black and the white peoples into a new social order. *For the truly marginal person, tribal history is important,* but tribal history is important only *as a way leading to the establishment of the fullness of humanity.* The marginal person tests himself on humanity [Buber 1961, p 168]. One has found his or her real identity when one is no longer fearful of losing it. This concept of the marginal person differs from that of the stranger in a strange land, which is the current popular meaning of marginality.

CHAPTER 6

SEGREGATION AND SEPARATISM VS POWER AND PARTICIPATION

Black separatism was briefly mentioned earlier. It will be examined in more detail in this chapter—as a function of white racism. White racism and black separatism are related to each other in a symbiotic way, with white racism being the action and black separatism being the reaction.

Black separatism, therefore, should be viewed for what it is—a judgment concerning the presence of white racism. Black separatism is not something that exists by itself. It should not be exalted as an ideological banner to be fol-

56

lowed and a desirable goal to be accomplished. Essential-
ly black separatism is an example of failure in relationships
between blacks and the society at large that was mentioned
by Gardner, as we noted in Chapter 2. Because white
racism continues to exist, we may have to live with and
accept black separatism for some time to come.

Thus black separatism, which is a response to white racism, is a movement that the public should strive to understand without endorsing it or opposing it. As we stated
in Chapter 1, any group has the right to withdraw, especially if withdrawal appears to be the only way of avoiding
utter frustration and humiliation.

Separatism may contribute to racial unity, but ultimately
it has a destructive side effect of social disorganization in a
pluralistic setting. As stated by Reuel Howe, "Inclusion is
the only way in which one can achieve wholeness" [Howe
1971, p 31]. History records a harvest of bitter fruit result-
ing from separation, alienation, and estrangement: riot,
plagues, poverty, disease, death, and destruction. These
are the consequences of segregation and separatism, which
eventually result in discrimination.

SOCIOLOGY AND SEPARATISM

Some advocates of separatism call for organizations that
are made up of one race only—that are racially homogeneous associations that exclude others who are different.
The most effective social movements in history, however,
are those which are pragmatic and inclusive and not those
that are ideological and exclusive. That is the sociologist's
way of saying that the most effective social movements
are those which set forth achievable goals and workable
programs and which include all kinds of people who are
interested in these goals and programs. On the other hand,
movements die out if they are based only on ideology and
myth and exclude all but a limited class. Howe has labeled
exclusionist groups as defensive [Howe 1971, p 26]. They
tend to exclude persons whom they do not understand and
persons of whom they are afraid.

The number of people available to participate in a social
movement is an important power resource. The inclusion-

ist principle of social organization increases the power potential of numbers, and the exclusionist principle limits this resource. When power blocs are composed of people who have come together because of a common concern, then these power blocs are flexible. Such groups can increase their power by expanding their numbers.

A basic principle about power relationships is that any clustering of power will tend to generate countervailing centers of power that in turn tend to balance the original cluster of power. If a power struggle initiated by blacks is put on a strictly racial basis, the countervailing power of the white majority in America is overwhelming. So the black minority is beaten from the beginning.

For minorities, power (and especially the power of numbers) develops from coalitions and alliances. It is inappropriate to limit, before an issue arises, the kinds of people with whom you will and will not establish alliances. As situations arise, you can determine the compatibility of potential allies. We make a mistake if we decide to exclude people as a matter of policy or ideology before the situation presents itself. When power blocs are organized along racial lines, the possibility for alliances is absent. Rigidity tends to set in.

Consider the increasing cooperation between the United States and the Union of the Soviet Socialist Republics as well as the alliance between the United States and Japan. These are illustrations of power blocs that are organized around common interests and pragmatic concerns, rather than being organized around a common race of people. Such power blocs are flexible and can change according to changing circumstances

On the other hand, the USSR and China are more likely in their relationships to be guided by ideology, and these two are growing apart.

To freeze the existing race relations situation in the United States into separate black and white molds may provide some immediate psychological release for persons who are not wise in the ways of social change, but it does not provide the flexibility necessary for the rearrangement of power blocs as new circumstances develop.

RECOGNIZING WHAT
THE SEPARATIST MOVEMENT
REALLY IS

We cannot bring about reconciliation by perpetuating separation, no matter how attractive separatism may be in the short run. Separatism is beneficial only as a temporary means of negotiating participation in the society at large. Any other separatist arrangement clearly is protective and defensive and is a signal to the adversary that those who have withdrawn feel that they are inadequate. Careful biographies of fanatical segregationist leaders, such as Adolph Hitler, reveal that they believe themselves to be inadequate.

The current state of affairs among black and white people is an example of a principle set forth by Alexander Leighton, psychiatrist and anthropologist, shortly after the end of the Second World War. He said.

> Where stress is severe and social disorganization is extensive, the breakdown-and-repair process is likely to take a violent form consisting in groups of people, each coalesced around a different system of belief, struggling with each other until one group dominates or until an equilibrium is achieved among several dominant groups [Leighton 1948, p 332].

In recent years the stress has been particularly severe for black people; the social disorganization in the slums is real. Black people have been pushed back from participating in the mainstream of this society and have not been aided in overcoming dehumanizing poverty. This has happened at a time when the nation as a whole was more aware of the burdens of its disadvantaged members, was better able to share the burdens, but tended to practice benign neglect.

I see the black separatist movement, then, as a harvest of the bitter fruit of fragmentation in the civil rights movement caused by despair, broken promises, and unfulfilled hopes.

The black separatist movement must be recognized for what it is: a negative judgment against the racism of the middle-class white majority.   For the sake of blacks, as well as whites, it must not be exalted as something which is positive and good.   To endorse the black separatist movement and its eventual consequence of racial estrangement is a denial of the mutual responsibility and interdependence of black and white people, of rich and poor people. Moreover, such an endorsement is but another way of approving the white segregationist movement of the past. That has brought disunity and disorder to this nation.   The black separatist movement will bring more disunity and disorder.

THE REASON FOR COMMUNITY

The essential purpose of this chapter has been to show the doubtful long-term benefits which may result from organizing society around exclusive racial and ethnic power blocs.

One reason that people cluster and come together in a community is to gain mutual benefit and protection. In a community people can have easy access to each other. One person is available to do for another what the other cannot do for himself or herself. There is a necessary interdependence in all life, city life and country life.

In our present and past practices of ghettoization and social discrimination, people have been separated who need each other, particularly black, brown, and white people. Death, disease, distrust, and disorder have resulted from these separations and have adversely affected the quality of life in this society.

Ghettoization and community are not the same.

To organize society around racial and ethnic groups is to exclude people who do not belong to these groups. No racial or ethnic group is self-sufficient.   Thus, to organize society along racial power blocs is to raise unnecessary barriers to human interaction and human community where people need each other.

RETRIBALIZATION

The attempt to organize society into black and white power blocs is an attempt to retribalize society.   The tribe, historically, has suffered from the in-group and out-group syndrome with its emphasis on *our* people and *those* people. What usually follows is the judgment that our people (the in-group) are good, and those people (the out-group) are bad. Such a judgment then becomes the basis of fear and suspicion, hostility and hate. Opportunities to know and understand each other are cut off. Violence is often the outcome.

The records of modern and ancient societies support this conclusion. Within recent years, Nigeria was plunged into a devastating civil war because of ancient tribal hostilities. Tribal hostilities were at the root of the war in Bangladesh.

The tribe (racial, ethnic, or national) has been exalted as the source of identity and pride. Most tribes perform these functions for their members up to a certain point, although in the last analysis it is the outsider who expands the range of our identity (see the discussion in Chapters 2 and 4). In addition to the positive contributions of the tribe, however, the tribes are also the source of hostility and hate for others. Most advocates of tribal unity tend to emphasize the positive and ignore these negative aspects of tribal life.

The negatives of retribalization will not go away, however. They parade their products upon an international stage in view of all; for example, civil warfare between the ethnic tribes in Nigeria, summer warfare between the racial tribes in the United States, periodic warfare since at least 1300 BC between the nation-state tribes in the Near East. When we weigh the advantages and disadvantages of tribal life, we must conclude that the negative consequences ultimately outweigh the positive benefits.

Power is the capacity to induce another to change his behavior in a prescribed way. Racial inequality and discrimination in the United States have weakened this nation. If people who practice these demeaning activities are to change, people who want the change must have sufficient power to induce others to behave in another prescribed way. Such power is most effective when it is exercised by organizations, associations, and institutions in the community in which people of all racial and ethnic backgrounds can participate [Willie 1969a, ch 3]. People are the ultimate source of human power. Because it is foolhardy to cut oneself off from power, it is foolish to cut oneself off from the people, all of the people. We need people power; blacks as well as whites need it. People are especially powerful when they work together in groups to achieve a common goal. And the groups are especially powerful when they are made up of people from different backgrounds.

INCREASED PARTICIPATION IN POWER STRUCTURES

If power in human society ultimately rests in the people, any pattern of social organization which increases human concern, involvement, accessibility, and assistance is empowering. Thus what is needed is increased opportunities for participation by black and other minority peoples in the organizations, associations, and institutions of societies.

By participation with other people, black people will gain more power than they ever could obtain by separating from whites into an exclusive racial tribe. Any separatist movement is self-limiting to the power of the people included in the separating tribe. Structures that are designed to help bring about worldwide cooperation and unity have not been fully effective so far. The United Nations, in spite of very slow progress in many fields, has made significant contributions in many other fields, and we hope that the member nations may be able to make necessary changes before the United Nations becomes ineffective. Attempts to form and maintain such international structures are a recognition of the ultimate source of power—the people, all of the people, united. Power reposes in all of the people and cannot be limited to black groups or white groups.

CHAPTER 7

PLURALISM
AND INTERDEPENDENCE

We are called to be interdependent, whether we like it or not. We are grafted together in a complementary fashion so that each completes the other. This is the nature of social systems, including local communities and national societies.

COMPENSATING AND COMPLEMENTING

Of course a person can exist with one eye, one arm, one leg, and even one kidney or one lung. But such a person is not physically complete. The miracle of life is that it does enable parts of our physical and social systems to compensate for those parts that are inadequate or absent.

We should not, however, mistake compensatory action for complementary action. Compensation is the correction for organic loss in one part of the body by increased functioning of another part of the same body. In complementary action, however, there is a mutual give and take in which each part supplies what is lacking in the other and thereby completes the organism or system so that it may function with fullness. In compensating action, the strong give to the weak and the weak receive from the strong. But in complementary action, all are at once strong and weak, each giving and receiving according to the requirements of the situation. Much of what passes for complementary action is in fact compensatory and therefore not true interdependence.

Many of us have failed to recognize and accept our interdependence because we have failed to realize that independence is not a virtue and dependence is not a vice. At some period in our life, we all must experience each, independence and dependence.

FAIR SHARE AND
AND THE
SURVIVAL OF THE FITTEST

We should place this discussion within the framework of our contemporary crisis in community life and the growing estrangement between dominants and subdominants, that is, the estrangement between young and old, poor and rich, black and white people. Peace may be restored and reconciliation achieved in our communities and associations only if we can recognize our interdependence.

When younger people, poor people, and black people are deprived of a relationship with older people, rich people, and white people, the former cannot learn from the latter how to be humble and generous, which are characteristic actions of dominant people of good will. By the same token, when older, affluent, and white people are cut off from and deprived of a relationship with younger, poor, and black people, the dominants cannot learn from the subdominants how to be courageous and magnanimous, which are characteristic actions of subdominant people of good will. Each category of people in our society has had experiences which others could learn and profit from.

Because poor people have had limited resources, they have had few opportunities to practice generosity. The rich people could teach the poor the importance, even the necessity, of being generous, of giving more than is required.

The graduates of my alma mater, Morehouse College, come predominantly from poor black families. The information from Morehouse College indicates that the poor have not learned yet how to be genuinely generous. Only about one-sixth of the alumni in recent years have made annual contributions. Generosity is as necessary for the poor as for the rich in affirming themselves and in implementing goals for the welfare of others.

Because rich people have been in the driver's seat and have focused their attention largely on growth, expansion, and progress, they have had little time to think about magnanimous activities, of taking less than they are entitled to have. The citizens of our more wealthy states, like New York and Massachusetts, complain if the amount of federal funds returned to their state is less than what the state residents paid out in federal taxes. The poor, who have suffered long and who have learned how to make do with less than what they are entitled to, could teach the rich the meaning and necessity of magnanimity in community life.

Giving and getting one's fair share has become an endemic slogan for all sectors of the population. This slogan is appropriate for a mechanical order or a society governed by instinct, but not for an interdependent community of people.

The survival of the fittest may be the operational law of the animal kingdom, but it is an inappropriate principle on which to base interaction in the human community. For humans, we must ask, "What is fittest?" and "Fittest for what?" It could be that persons who have learned how to accept their dependent status are most fit to survive. Throughout life, many people have difficulty accepting the fact that they are not self-sufficient. Perhaps one of the most important lessons that we must learn is that we are dependent.

Psychiatrist Edward Stainbrook in a lecture at the Up-
state Medical Center in Syracuse, New York, once made
this simple but profound statement, that people can be
helped only by people. And Jane Jacobs has reminded us
that our safety and security are guaranteed not so much by
the protective physical barriers that we erect around ourselves but by the presence of other people [Jacobs 1961,
pp 30-32].

Interdependence, then, does not denote a kind of stand-
off condition consisting, as it were, of protective moral
tariffs where members of dominant or subdominant groups
determine for themselves what is appropriate for another.
Interdependence involves living together in community and
each doing for others what the others cannot do for themselves. It is fine to exhort all people to dwell together.
However, it is probably more responsible to discover why
communities have fractioned and how people have come
to look on others as aliens and strangers. In the long run
this probably explains why we have international wars.

IS LIFE JUST ANOTHER EQUATION?

Most of us tend to approach life and its problems as
if human life were an equation in which a is always bal-
anced by b. How often have we talked about "the human
equation"? The equation, then, is a frame of reference
which some of us use as a crutch to help us understand
community issues. If we are not careful, we make mistakes when we oversimplify society or the social system,
especially when we compare it to a mechanical system.

At mid-century, for example, when extremist organizations like the White Citizens Councils made their appear-
ance on the American scene, harassing blacks, many people
were dead sure that the extremist white racist organizations like these were formed as a way of countering the
demands of black organizations. It was common practice
for public officials and newspaper editorials to be against
extremism in American life. Among the extremist organizations usually mentioned were the White Citizens Council
on the one hand and the National Association for the Ad-
vancement of Colored People on the other. Only a dis-

torted frame of reference and a total lack of knowledge about the activities of the two organizations could seek to balance NAACP against the White Citizens Council. Yet in the opinion of many these two organizations tended to generate each other and were equally to blame as extremists. Such a wrong conclusion arose because some people used the equation as their frame of reference. By looking at society that way, a white organization always came into being to deal with the activities of a black organization and vice versa. A threat was always assumed and thus the action was justified as reaction.

Thomas Pettigrew also fell prey to the tendency to organize his thoughts about black-white relations in the United States in the image of an equation. In his book *A Profile of the Negro American,* Pettigrew casts blacks and whites into a symbiotic relationship. He points out, for example, that the tendency for whites to "flatter themselves into the conviction that they are in fact 'superior' " is related to "deferential behavior of the role-playing Negro . . ." [Pettigrew 1964, p 5].

I do not see the relationship as one of cause and effect. A person can experience discrimination and oppression without believing that he is in fact inferior even though the oppressors may believe that they are superior. Pettigrew has attempted to balance the pathology of asserted superiority by some white Americans with the pathology of acknowledged inferiority by some black Americans. He has further suggested that one form of pathology tends to generate the other.

If race relations in the United States were an equation and if the black-white interaction could indeed be explained in cause-and-effect terms, then whites ought to have stopped acting as if they were superior when confronted with nondeferential blacks. The arrogant white responses to the fearless marchers led by Martin Luther King, Jr, in Alabama linger in our memory, and so is the haughty federal government's response to the courageous poor people and their campaign in Resurrection City in the District of Columbia after King's death. The marching black people and the campaigning poor people were courageous.

They did not act as if they were inferior. They were not deferent. They were not pathological. Yet their adversaries continued to act as if they were superior to the poor and the black and publicly acted out the pathological behavior that is associated with a false sense of superiority. The record shows that some people act as if they are superior even when those whom they oppress do not act as if they are inferior.

Although Pettigrew uses the imagery of the equation to analyze and explain black-white relations in the United States, he is not unmindful of the absurdities to which it can lead. To illustrate, he says,

> The segregationist creates Negro disorganization with his creed, then turns around and justifies his creed in terms of Negro disorganization . . . . In this sense, the segregationist resembles the young boy who in cold blood grabbed a double-barrelled shotgun, killed his father with one blast, then whirled the gun around and killed his mother with the other. When brought to trial for the double murder, he pleaded for mercy on the grounds that he was an orphan [Pettigrew 1964, p 160].*

This, then, is the error of looking at life as if it were an equation. We tend to absolve ourselves of problems that may be of our own making; we tend too often and too easily to attribute to others our own shortcomings. When we look upon life as an equation, then people, places, and things become assets or liabilities to balance against each other. But the human community is not mechanical and cannot be treated this way. The members of an equation are components in a collectivity, rather than being citizens of a community. The members of an equation occupy spaces, fill slots, and hold positions that balance each other.

When life is approached as a human equation, we are obsessed with the kinds and categories of people in our communities and in our associations. We agonize and debate about the tipping point and speculate about the ratio

*A Profile of the American Negro by T F Pettigrew © 1964. Reprinted by permission of D. Van Nostrand Company.

of black to white members that an organization can tolerate. When life is viewed as an equation, we speak fearfully and forebodingly about the chances of survival in a changing residential area rather than rejoicing hopefully about the enrichment and creativity that can arise from diversity.

THE DEATH
OF THE PARISH

For example, in Syracuse, New York, there was news of another church that bit the dust. Reporter Ramona Baxter Bowden of *The Syracuse Post Standard* called her article "A Requiem for a Church." She reported that Danforth United Church, which was first organized in 1884, would close its doors at the end of 1968. The Christian Church of the Disciples of Christ and Danforth Congregational Church had united in 1930. Its pastor, the Rev Howard Horn, had been at Danforth United Church since 1962. He said, "Community change . . . caught up with the church with the result that . . . the congregation voted to dissolve as a church corporation, directing its board of trustees to dispose of all property and other assets . . . ." Reporter Bowden said, "In spite of the altering neighborhood, the congregation had decided to remain in its present location and invested $90,000 for repairs and remodeling. But even this outlay was not enough to stem the ebbing tide of a diminishing congregation" [Bowden 1968, p 3].

The story of the Danforth United Church is legion. Other churches with predominantly white congregations, like Danforth, have experienced similar fates. The news announcing the demise of such churches is never complete. For example, the cause of death is never reported; only the circumstances such as a "changing community" are alluded to. Why should a church in a changing area die if the characteristics of its membership also are changing so that the church membership reflects the characteristics of the people in the changing area? Why would a parish die if it were helping troubled, frightened, and weary people, if it were a setting for interdependent relationships?

If life is viewed as an equation, white churches must always die when white members move away. This, in effect, is what the reporter said: "Old families died and young groups escaped to the suburbs" [Bowden 1968]. Yet there were plenty of black people and poor people and young people nearby. Why could not that church attract them and continue to exist as a worshiping community enriched with the diversity of its new members? The reporter concluded her requiem with this statement: "Mr. Horn has done such a valiant job of relating to the community that his church has been swallowed up . . . ." One wonders why the swallowing was not the other way around, why the church did not swallow its changing and new community. By doing this, it would have become a parish of marginal people with each person trying to understand the way of life of persons unlike himself or herself. There probably would have been tension in such a parish. But it might have survived. As it so happened, the Danforth Church continued largely as an organization of like-minded and look-alike people, and in the end it failed to survive because it failed to become a diversified congregation in a changing and pluralistic neighborhood.

UNMIXED INSTITUTIONS IN MIXED COMMUNITIES

These observations on the death of a parish lead to a concluding observation. Neighborhood institutions such as churches, schools, and other associations are becoming increasingly homogeneous in the persons who participate in them, and this is happening at a time when the metropolitan community is more heterogeneous: the community institutions serve unmixed groups while the community is becoming more and more mixed. These two trends are on a collision course.

What can we do to deal with this situation? We must learn how to live as marginal people with diversity, which is part of the modern community. Marginality brings forth coherence and meaning through interdependence.

In Chapter 5, we referred to Harvey Cox's statement that the Jews probably came closest to fulfilling their calling when they were wandering. This idea is appropriate to recall at this point. The wandering Jewish people demonstrated to the world that they could participate in and adapt to a variety of nation states, communities, and cultural groups and yet maintain and affirm a moral and ethical belief system essential to their identity. The history of the Jewish people, as mentioned in Chapter 5, is an excellent example of the creative contribution of marginal people on a world scale. The Jewish people lived the interdependent life wherever they wandered, giving and receiving from each community, as indicated in Chapters 4 and 5.

CHAPTER 8

RACIAL HATRED AND
RECONCILIATION
– A WORLD PERSPECTIVE

In the summer of 1968, I had the high privilege of going to Coventry, England, to attend an international conference on People and Cities. I would like to share with you some of the information and insights obtained from that conference in order to give an international perspective to the issues that are discussed in this book.

The conference convened from June 25 through July 2, 1968, at Coventry Cathedral. The excitement of the conference came not only from the subject matter discussed but also from the kinds of people who participated and the setting in which the conference met.

THE DISASTER THAT WAS AN OPPORTUNITY

Coventry has been described as "both an ancient city with a long history and a twentieth century city looking to the future." The significant history for Coventry goes back to the eleventh century when, once before, it knew destruction. According to a general information bulletin prepared by the municipality, "The Danes, early in the eleventh century, destroyed a nunnery in Coventry on the site of which in 1043 AD Leofric, Earl of Mercia, and his wife, Godiva, founded a Benedictine Monastery, succeeded on the same site by Coventry's first Cathedral."

Coventry is an industrial city manufacturing several products, including automobiles, that are marketed around the world. The Coventry population is approximately one-third of a million. Coventry, of course, is not one of the largest cities in Great Britain. But it is one of the most outstanding. Like several other European cities, Coventry was blitzed in 1940. The city center was destroyed.

Unlike several other cities, however, Coventry did not rebuild in the image of the city that was fallen. It took advantage of the disastrous circumstances to start anew. Today it is not uncommon to hear public officials describe the disaster from the war blitz as an opportunity. What they mean is that the event gave Coventry the opportunity to rebuild a city for people, to create an environment that is attractive and convenient for working, shopping, living, entertainment, and recreation.

Coventry is noted for more, however, than its radical redevelopment plan. Coventry is well known because of its cathedral. Before the smoldering ashes had cooled, there was immediate resolve to rebuild the Cathedral Church of Saint Michael after it had been reduced to ruins by fire bombs one Thursday night in November, the 14th, it was, in 1940. Great Britain and Germany were at war, and Germany was fighting to win.

According to the Cathedral Provost, on that fateful date "Coventry suffered the longest air-raid of any one night on any British city." These were the consequences: scores of people were maimed and killed, and a great cathedral was reduced to ruins.

But out of this tragedy grew the new Cathedral Church of Saint Michael, which was consecrated May 25, 1962, in the presence of Her Majesty the Queen. It is a masterpiece in modernity, a spacious structure with a roof 80 feet high and slender uniform concrete columns supporting the ceiling, 5 majestic stained glass windows in each aisle of the nave plus a great baptistry window containing 198 separate panes of stained glass reflecting upon a huge sandstone boulder from the valley Barakat near Bethlehem in Jordan, which serves as the baptismal basin.

The new church is a witness to the spirit of renewal which characterizes the city, and this church is appropriately called "Coventry Cathedral."

There is more than this bright, shining, new, and modern structure. The ruins of the old have been left standing, and they are joined to the new church by an arch. The ruins are symbolic. To some, they signify hope and life. People point to the new church as a manifestation. To others, they memorialize death and destruction. People look at what happened as an indication of what war is. Both reactions to the ruins are valid.

THE CHARRED CROSS OF COVENTRY

But the ruins are more than a sign or symbol. In the ruins are recorded the spirit of a people. It is not the spirit of enterprise and innovation. These are found in several other places. The spirit of forgiveness in Coventry has made it an inspiration to the world. Some thoughtful person tied together by wire two irregular pieces of the burned roof beams from the destroyed cathedral and placed them in the east end of the ruins. The Charred Cross of Coventry has become world famous. More important are the words on the wall carved deep and high behind the Charred Cross. The words are simple and clear:

FATHER FORGIVE

This is the message in Coventry which keeps motivating that city and the rest of the world, which makes the "fire in Coventry" a continuous flame and not just a sad event of the past. It is a fire that continues to destroy the old that has become useless in order to make way for the new.

The forgiveness which destroys old hatreds is a living presence in Coventry in the undercroft of the cathedral ruins. A lounge has been fashioned there for international students where they may meet and become acquainted with each other. Refreshments are provided and the opportunity to read or to participate in good conversation is afforded. This lounge is maintained by people from Germany, a people who were fighting to win on that fateful night. The hostess, a German woman, called the lounge and its maintenance an act of reconciliation. But such an action could never have been expressed without the prior expression of forgiveness.

DIFFERENT CAREERS
FROM DIFFERENT COUNTRIES

The People and Cities Conference was held during the celebration of the golden jubilee of the refounding of the ancient Diocese of Coventry. Three years of preparation preceded the conference. Several workshops had been held in more than twenty different cities throughout the world. These workshops had defined issues, identified problems, and raised questions with which the assembled conference attempted to deal. The issues of *social differentiation* and *social participation* emerged as the two most significant with which people in the conference should deal.

The conference delegates numbered more than 150 and came from 35 countries. They were organized into small groups to wrestle with these issues. Actually the small groups were the heart of the conference. We came to know each other by exposing our ideas and attitudes and by sharing and exchanging information. I was in group Number Thirteen. It was led by a conference participant from India. Also in this group were a woman social scientist from Germany, a businessman from India, an architect from Brazil, and four citizens of Great Britain—a clergyman, the political editor for a daily newspaper, a school headmaster, and a political scientist. Such a combination meant that all ideas expressed were examined from international and interdisciplinary perspectives.

THE VALUE
OF GROUP CONSENSUS

There were differences to be sure, which in part were associated with the various value systems of the participants. The differing systems of beliefs in turn were a function of the nations and cultures that participants represented.

In spite of these differences, group members arrived at a consensus about some principles for community life. Consensus emerging from such a group setting is significant and something of value. My group wrestled with the issue of participation in community life and came up with the following conclusions:

≫1. Participation has intrinsic value as a self-corrective in human associations.

≫2. The best way to learn about participation is by participating. There is no real education for participation.

≫3. Participation is directly in proportion to the degree of communication within an organization.

≫4. Effective participation in the community involves an interaction between individuals at the grass-roots level and groups of individuals at the intermediate level which have the power to influence the larger social system.

Another small group spoke directly about violence in the city and came to the conclusion that

> violence will generally occur where no dialogue exists between social groups and authorities.

This conclusion suggests the further idea that the possibility for disorder in the community increases as communication and participation among the people decrease.

CONCLUSIONS
LACED WITH QUALIFIERS

The groups were less forthright in their analysis of social differentiation in the city. Conclusions were tentative and laced with qualifiers. Among the ideas mentioned were the following [Pattey 1968]:

> We have to ask what it is that divides man from man, ... and to discover whether these divisions are always harmful.
> Division in society does not always imply hostility or dissention.
> We need to discover which divisions are creative.
> We need to see how far division in society can go before it becomes harmful.

These, as you may recognize, were masterful statements of indecision. One group got around to discussing slums, but again the conclusions were indecisive. Group members said something like this:

Many people are concentrated in slums because they cannot escape. But there are some who do not want to for fear of losing their social identity.

In short, the conference said a little bit of this and a little bit of that about the divisions within society as if they were inconsequential. In fact, however, the divisions between humankind are probably the most troubling experiences of our times. Reports on the workshops preliminary to the conference were prepared by Sociologist David Boswell of the University of Manchester. He took note of the economic, racial, ethnic, and religious differences among the peoples within societies and reminded us that these differentiations are not new.

"But what is new," Professor Boswell pointed out, "is the . . . annual account of the richest and strongest country in the modern world at war with itself" because of these divisions within its population. This reference was to the United States and the massive disruptions within its cities during the 1960s.

FAILURE TO DEAL WITH SOCIETY'S DIFFERENCES

One can only speculate why the conference failed to adequately deal with the problem of social differentiation. One reason might be that the conference planners took the advice of the sociologist who summarized the workshop reports. He admitted that "factors associated with . . . social divisions formed the bulk of the contents of the reports," and distinct references were made about the divisions between the rich and the poor and between the exploiters and the exploited, particularly in the workshops that had been held in the Third World—the nations of Africa, South America, and Asia. But Professor Boswell recommended that the conference deal with issues and situations common to all urban areas in different parts of the world.

Thus the subject matter arousing passion was not high-
lighted.

Also it is probable that a fundamental confrontation did
not take place over the issues of injustice, inequality, and
social differentiation because of the composition of the
delegate body. It was a privilege to meet and greet people
from Ghana, India, Israel, South Africa, Argentina, Brazil,
Australia, Canada, Japan, Thailand, Czechoslovakia, Germany, Uganda, Zambia, Great Britain, and other countries,
But most of these people were middle class—professors,
architects, city planners, clergymen, government officials,
physicians, businessmen, and students. Most were affiliated
with the governmental, economic, educational, and religious establishments in their country, and they analyzed
problems from the *dominant,* not the *subdominant,* point
of view.

LORDS AND LADIES
SERVING THE WORKERS

The Right Honorable the Earl of March and Kinrava, the
conference chairman, who performed in an able way, il-
luminated this problem of the assembly, namely, the composition of the delegate body. Jokingly he said that he
did not often discuss revolutions because, if and when a
revolution should come, with a name like his, he would
be among the first to be strung up. This remark received
howling laughter from the audience. Lord March continued his story by stating that a worker and trade union
official informed him that the Right Honorable Earl need
not fear such a happening. Hanging was the old method
that had been found to be ineffective. The new regime
would find it more beneficial, said the trade unionist, to
use the high status members of the old regime in the service of the revolutionaries and that Lord March could look
forward to a good life of fine service to the workers if a
revolution ever should occur.

This story was told in passing and added fun and levity
to the affair before a more serious topic was introduced.
The issue that I highlight is not the story. The story was
fictitious and funny and achieved its purpose.

What was wrong was that it had to be told by Lord March. The workers were not present to speak for themselves.

The kinds of people invited to participate have a great deal to do with what topics are discussed and how they are discussed. This principle applies not only to conferences but also to local community associations.

THE ONE-WAY STREET
OF THE DOMINANTS

In spite of the fact that subdominants were not present to speak in their own behalf, several participants spoke about the presence of injustice and inequality in the world. These people spoke about their concern during the final plenary session when delegates were invited to speak from the floor about their reactions to the conference summary and about what they planned to do to implement ideas and insights derived from the conference.

One would be in error if he suggested that the conference did not deal with gut issues. But people like a participant from Argentina felt that the priorities were all mixed up. For instance, one paragraph in the conference summary, prepared by the Dean of Liverpool, was devoted to the Third World, and even that single paragraph temporized with the issues. I quote that paragraph so that you may judge for yourself how limited was its perspective [Pattey 1968, p 9]:

There was not much emphasis on the world scale in the reports from the groups, though this is not to say that this dimension was absent from the Conference itself. However, some groups gave consideration to a comparison between the needs of the third world and those of the developed countries. Many members of the Conference have remarked that on their overall impression they have gained that the problems of people and cities are much the same the whole world over. But obviously in some areas much more practical help is needed if participation is to become a reality. One report suggested that a fund should be earmarked to help indigenous groups to speak out on issues which concern them. Another group reported that whilst it was acknowledged that it was "trade not aid" that was wanted, could one expect nations to act other than in self-interest alone? Is the only course to show the developed countries that help (trade, etc.) with developing countries is in their long-term interest? Is this another aspect of Social Science not keeping pace with technology? There is a need for critical groups to protest and to make public opinion aware. The Churches should be free to do this, and should be less introverted.

Such a paragraph does not conjure up an image of the Church's making no peace with oppression and doing battle in behalf of the poor, oppressed, and afflicted or reconciling the nations. Apparently the groups did not arrive at any real understanding of interdependence.

One gets the impression that the developed nations still view their involvement with developing nations as a one-way street in which the strong help the weak on the terms of the strong.

The delegate from Argentina was Professor of Church and Community Social Ethics in Buenos Aires. He took exception to the attempt to even up situations and trim off the rough edges that differentiate [Willie 1968, pp 11-12]. In an impassioned speech from the floor which opened the conference to public debate and a fundamental exchange, he stated that we are in for trouble if we do not recognize the problems of poverty and the tottering economic systems in the Third World, which continues to be weak because of the trading policies and practices of developed nations. In the developing nations, he said, people will not subscribe to the principles of Christianity or any other religion when they are hungry. We should give priority to finding ways of feeding the hungry people of the world. It is not enough to deal with the problems of the Third World in a passing reference, he concluded.

My own sentiments were in accord with those of the Argentine professor. I publicly endorsed his position and also called attention to a passage in the Conference Summary which stated that some people concentrated in slums do not want to escape for fear of losing their social identity. I suggested that we should be slow to conclude that slum people like slums if we too are not slum dwellers. I elaborated on the dangers involved in projecting one's own ideas and feelings upon others. Finally I pointed out that our information and interpretations of the desires of poor people would have been much better had poor people been present in the conference to speak for themselves, to tell us whether they do or do not prefer to live in slums. Several participants and some of the conference officials concurred with the idea that the delegate body should have been more diversified, particularly in representation from varying social classes and income groups. Not only should the principle of diversification be followed in the practice of inviting delegates, they said, but also in the composition of community decision-making councils.

The conference faced the issues of participation but was found wanting in dealing with the issues of social differentiation.

ISRAELI MEETS EGYPTIAN

The opportunity to meet people from different nations is sometimes more significant than the ideas discussed in formal sessions. A delegate from Israel illustrated this point. Though much was left unsaid, one felt the depth of his involvement and was moved with genuine sentiments of pathos and admiration as this delegate from Israel spontaneously told the assembly about his Sunday morning accidental meeting with a lad from Egypt in the Cathedral ruins while most Christian members of the conference were attending church in and around Coventry. He told about how they talked for more than three hours. He offered this experience as an example of the meeting between people that the conference had accomplished. The Israeli delegate's testimony was one that many could have given. My table talk with a white South African had similar overtones.

Although the small groups which were the heart of the conference did not adequately deal with the Third World, plenary sessions did include three informative presentations by conference participants from developing nations in Asia, Africa, and Latin America.

ONE WATER TAP
PER FIFTY PEOPLE

Mr K C Sivaramakrishna, Chief Executive, Durgapur Development Authority, lectured on the problems of India and that part of the world [Willie 1968, p 17]. Mr Sivaramakrishna focused on Calcutta. He said that the Calcutta Metropolitan District has a population of 7,000,000 and a land area of 490 square miles. This means that Calcutta has a density of more than 14,000 persons per square mile.

According to Mr Sivaramakrishna, classical land control methods cannot be used in planning and redeveloping Calcutta because of the many different municipalities and other political divisions within the Metropolitan District. Thus a functional approach was tried, focusing on water, sanitation and drainage, and transportation. To coordinate these functional efforts, several authorities have been created which transcend local authority. While metropolitan government hardly would be acceptable in a country that jealously guards local prerogatives, a Metropolitan Water and Sanitation Authority and a Metropolitan Transport and Traffic Authority were acceptable. These authorities were coordinated by capital budgeting and fiscal control by a Metropolitan Planning and Development Authority, a state government agency. According to Mr Sivaramakrishna, this approach to planning came about largely because of the cholera epidemic of 1958 which claimed 900 lives. The World Health Organization entered the picture then and recommended that a massive environmental improvement program should be undertaken.

It is a group of modest programs that Mr Sivaramakrishna would like to introduce. He would like to start some kind of street system and put in water taps at the rate of one to every 50 persons, community latrines at the rate of one to every 50 families, remove the contaminated tanks and close them, gradually extend the sewage system which is now limited to the central section of Calcutta.

If only there were more money! He said that, at the rate that housing funds are being made available, it would take 120 years to clear and rehouse half of the slums. Mr Siva-ramakrishna is looking for a breakthrough before cynicism sets in. At present, he can say only that the city is in a mess.

MIGRATION AND POWER
IN SOUTH AMERICA AND AFRICA

Mr Carlos Sabanes, Secretary, Urban Missions Program for Latin America in Argentina, spoke about the problems of Latin America [Willie 1968, pp 20-21]. It is not possible to understand the process of urbanization in Latin America, he said, if one does not dig down to the roots of the internal migrations, which are provoked or caused by a grossly inadequate structure based on what he called "the idolatrous cult of private property." Mr Sabanes said that, if the Church wishes to help the dispossessed, it must rise up and engage in a power struggle with the people of property in Latin America who exploit the poor. But then, he said, he did not expect the Church to do very much because the Church has always been afraid of power. "The most tragic aspect," he concluded, "is that in the eyes of the poor or dispossessed the ecclesiastic establishment or religious institutional structure appears to be [an] accomplice and [a] beneficiary of the existing situation." Mr Sabanes described the ecclesiastic establishment which exists in Latin America as one which offers "palliatives or spiritual escape hatches or tunnels."

Professor K E de Graft-Johnson, Sociologist, University of Ghana, spoke about "The Hopes and Aspirations of African Nationalism" [Willie 1968, p 21]. He said that Africa does not have many cities, that 80% of the population in most African countries is in agriculture. Although most cities in Africa are new, Professor de Graft-Johnson said that people continue to drift to the cities (and the rate of urban migration is likely to increase greatly in the future) "because power is there." Thus the problems of Africa are not so much urban problems as they are problems of independence and problems of economics. He said that "independence raised the expectations of many people."

"But unfortunately," added Professor de Graft-Johnson, "the achievements of independence have been rather modest. The real crux of the problem is that the resources are so utterly inadequate for the tasks that have to be done." The Ghanian sociologist related the problems of developing nations directly to the rest of the world.

"Unless we adjust the payment system of the world, the inequalities between the rich and the poor will continue." he said. He pictured developing countries as the producers of raw materials for the developed world. Also he reminded his listeners that African countries must take whatever price the developed nations will give for the raw materials. Finally he said, "African developing nations are not asking for charity; they are asking for a recognition that every worker is worthy of a decent wage."

INTERDEPENDENCE
OF CITIES AND IN CITIES

The idea of interdependence ran throughout the remarks of the three speakers. The idea of interdependence was best expressed by a clergyman from India and a famous planner from Greece who participated in the conference. The Reverend Harry Daniels, Secretary of the Urban and Industrial Mission, East Asian Christian Council, spoke.

"Thank God . . . the call is not just to the Churches but to all men to serve a common need," he said. "One therefore feels and believes the problems . . . portrayed are [not just] the planner's [problems] in Calcutta . . . or the Government of India, but . . . [are] our common problem[s] and that we share in trying to resolve [them]." The Reverend Mr Daniels of Asia further said, "We cannot ignore what happens in any one part of the world" [Willie 1968, p 18].

A similar idea was offered by Dr Constantinos Doxiadis, world-renowned planning consultant, whose Institute of Ekistics is located in Athens, Greece. Dr Doxiadis said that eventually all cities will be interconnected, will be part of the same system [Willie 1968, p 16].

There was not consensus in the conference. But the weight of evidence and opinion pointed in the direction of increasing economic opportunities for all people in all cities as a major goal, a first in the order of priorities.

Second, there is the need to establish a sense of community among the peoples of this world. The record will show that the rise and fall of great cities in the past is the story of the rise and fall of a sense of community among their inhabitants. A sense of community exists where the weak are courageous and the mighty are humble, where the rich and the poor give more than they are required to give and take less than they are entitled to receive. There is community where people acknowledge their interdependence and all participate in the governing of the community, which is dedicated not to the glory of a tribe or a clan but to the welfare of all the people.

CHAPTER 9

THE AGONY AND THE GLORY
OF A
MARGINAL MAN

Tuesday morning, April 9, 1968, my wife, Mary Sue, and I boarded a plane to Atlanta to attend the funeral of Martin Luther King, Jr, on the campus of Morehouse College, which is his and my alma mater.

We landed in Atlanta near noon. Lo and behold, a great transformation began to take place! We found ourselves participating not only in a funeral but also in a festival—a genuine folk festival.

The campus was flooded by people—150,000 people at Morehouse College. There was little if any real preparation for crowd control, and yet the crowd was controlled. Because of the heat and other circumstances, several people fainted, and they were given emergency attention. But few if any were weeping.

Indeed, it was a victorious and joyful affair. It was another occasion to march. This the people did, the rich and the poor, the black and the white, from urban and rural America, the politicians and the entertainers, including several stewardesses from American Airlines dressed in their brightly colored uniforms. Yes, all sorts and conditions were there—men and women, boys and girls, walking up and down the campus while the funeral service was in progress. Indeed, it was another occasion to march—to walk, to meet, and to greet people, to identify with humanity.

The people said, "Amen," "Yes, Lord," "Hallelujah." In short, they answered the preacher by shouting out these phrases of approval as a way of acknowledging the truth in the words that were spoken. This is an old and honorable practice of the folk, extending back to the days of the earliest Christians. Many times I have heard my own father speak out when the spirit moved him and when the preaching was good in a Christian Methodist Episcopal Church in Dallas, Texas, in which I was baptized. Answering the preacher is a traditional custom, especially in the black community, which indicates that the message is getting through.

But something new was added in the funeral service for Martin Luther King, Jr. The people began to applaud. They applauded after the introduction of Senator Robert Kennedy, after the singing of "Precious Lord" by Miss Mahalia Jackson, and during the eulogy delivered by Dr Benjamin E Mays. It was a funeral, to be sure, but unlike any funeral I have ever seen. Truly, also, it was a festival.

We went South to grieve with the family, but we didn't meet the widow. We went South to mourn the deceased, but we didn't see the casket. We went South to take part in the worship service, but we didn't see the rostrum. Our fine view was blocked by people perched on the rods underneath the platform for the television cameras. We went South to make our last march with Dr King from the church to the campus. But traffic was so snarled that we could only ride from the airport to the college.

The adversities and impossibilities were no occasion for disappointment, however. For what we did see was more than we could have imagined. We saw joyful people instead of people who were sad. We celebrated a new resurrection instead of a rite of passage for the dead. As the funeral ended and as old friends greeted each other on the college campus, I began to ponder the meaning of this momentus event.

I saw the whole Easter event enacted before my eyes between April 4th and April 9th. There it was—another crucifixion and another resurrection. Thursday we heard of the tragic death. Tuesday we saw the beginning of a new era. We saw the spirit of Dr King dwelling amongst the people.

I am not talking about anything that is mystical and obscure. I am talking about a spirit manifested in action.

How do you suppose we got to the airport from the city of Atlanta? We rode the city buses, which shuttled people all over Atlanta from the Morehouse College campus. Staffed with black and white drivers, the bus system refused to accept pay for the service it performed that day in transporting thousands of mourners.

Flash back in your memory for a moment, just twelve short years before. It was the publicly franchised city bus system in Montgomery, Alabama, which brought Dr King to the attention of the nation. In the bus boycott of 1956, he fought to eliminate racially discriminatory seating practices.

In 1968, as the Atlanta buses graciously served his followers, the thought occurred to me that Dr King not only had won but that another bus company had overcome. In this small act of the Atlanta bus system I saw a fulfillment of Dr King's dream, I saw the indwelling of his spirit, I saw the manifestation of love and mercy, I saw the beginning of reconciliation.

We learned something else in our pilgrimage to Atlanta. We learned about the meaning that this man had for the masses of people. Middle-class people are moved by words. But poor people believe in works. Martin Luther King, Jr, was a man who embodied both ideas and actions, both words and works. This is why *all* the people were caught up in his spirit—the rich and the poor, the young and the old.

It is a mistake to attribute his greatness to his attitudes about peace, love, and justice, which he expressed in such beautiful and wonderful words. It is necessary to recognize also the significance of his actions, particularly his marching actions and his demonstrations.

Plenty of people take part in demonstrations but still carry hate in their hearts. Then there are those who say that they love but who continue to bypass their neighbor in need. Martin Luther King, Jr, spoke meaningful words; he was an eloquent minister of the word. But he also performed mighty acts. He was an unrelenting protester against injustice. It is in the combination of his actions and ideas that his greatness lies.

The significance of Dr King's actions was driven home to us as we rode from the airport to the campus in a courtesy car. A Southern Christian Leadership Conference courtesy car was nothing more than a privately owned automobile driven by its owner, who had decided that this was the way he would help on that day; this was the action in which he would engage. The worship service had not quite ended at Ebenezer Baptist Church as we rode from the airport to the campus for the out-of-doors service that was to follow the one which was held in the church.

There were five or six people in that car: Mrs Leo Murphy, wife of the former Pastor of Bethany Baptist Church of Syracuse, who traveled with us, and a couple of men from California.

My wife and I were straining to hear the radio and the words which the Reverend Ralph Abernathy was speaking during the church service. But the driver was oblivious to our attempts to hear and to listen. He was excited over the new people he had met that day and was ecstatically engaged in good conversation, so he turned off the intruding radio. His car was where the action was. Words were of little effect. He was the kind of person for whom action meant more than words.

The unfinished business that the Reverend Dr King leaves for us is to bring attitudes and actions together so that words and work may become one. For in such unity we may find community and hope for the future of mankind.

Tuesday in Atlanta was both a funeral and a festival, the agony and the glory of a marginal man.

REFERENCES
to
Works Cited
in the
Text

REFERENCES

Allport, Gordon W 1958 *The Nature of Prejudice.* Garden City, New York: Doubleday

Barzun, Jacques 1965 *A Study in Superstition.* New York: Harper & Row, Torchbook

Bennett, Lerone 1964 *What Manner of Man?* Chicago: Johnson

Bowden, Ramona Baxter 1968 Last rites approach at Danforth Church. Syracuse, New York: *The Post-Standard,* Nov 16, 1968

Buber, Martin
   1955 *Between Man and Man.* Boston, Massachusetts: Beacon

   1957 *Pointing the Way,* ed and transl by Maurice S Friedman. New York: Harper & Row, Torchbook

   1958 *Moses, The Revelation and the Covenant.* New York: Harper & Row, Torchbook

   1961 *Two Types of Faith* New York: Harper & Row, Torchbook

   1963 *Israel and the World.* New York: Schocken, paperback

Canon, Walter B 1939 *The Wisdom of the Body.* New York: Norton

Carmichael, Stokely, *in* Miller, William Robert (1968) *Martin Luther King, Jr.* New York: Avon

Cohen, Arthur A 1957 *Martin Buber.* New York: Hillary House

Coleman, James 1968 Equality of educational opportunity. *Integrated Education* 6(5) Sept–Oct

Conant, James B 1961 *Slums and Suburbs.* New York: Macmillan

Cox, Harvey 1965 *The Secular City.* New York: Macmillan

Census, *see* U S Bureau of the Census

Diamond, Stanley 1965 Black farce, white lies. *Dissent* 12:474

Dubos, René
1968 *So Human an Animal.* New York: Scribner's
1972 *A God Within.* New York: Scribner's

Ellison, Ralph 1952 *The Invisible Man.* New York: New American Library, paperback. Hardcover and copyright, New York: Random House.

Feagin, Joe R 1967 Black women in the American work force, *in* Willie, Charles V (1967) *The Family Life of Black People.* Columbus, Ohio: Merrill

Freud, Sigmund 1939 *Moses and Monotheism.* New York: Random House, Vintage book

Gardner, John W 1968 *No Easy Victories.* New York: Harper & Row

Handlin, Oscar 1963 *The American People.* London, U K: Hutchinson & Co

Howe, Reuel 1971 *Survival Plus.* New York: Seabury Press

Jacobs, Jane 1961 *The Life and Death of Great American Cities.* New York: Random House, Vintage Book

Jensen, Arthur R 1969 How much can we boost IQ and scholastic achievement? *Environment, Heredity and Intelligence.* Cambridge, Massachusetts: *Harvard Educational Review,* Reprint Series No. 2

Kardiner, Abraham, and Ovesey 1962 *The Mark of Oppression.* Cleveland, Ohio: World

King, Martin Luther, Jr 1967 *Where Do We Go from Here: Chaos or Community?* Boston, Massachusetts: Beacon, paperback. Hardcover and copyright, New York: Harper & Row

Leighton, Alexander 1948 *The Governing of Men.* Princeton, New Jersey: Princeton University Press

Mays, Benjamin E
    1968   Address at funeral of Martin Luther King, Jr
    1969   *Disturbed about Max.* Richmond, Va: John Knox Press

Merton, Robert 1949 *Social Theory and Social Structure.* New York: The Free Press

Miller, William Robert 1968 *Martin Luther King, Jr.* New York: Avon, a Discus book

Park, Robert E 1937 Introduction *in* Everett V Stonequist (1937) *The Marginal Man.* New York: Scribner's

Pattey, Edward 1968 *in* Willie, Charles V (1968) Summary of the Report of the People and Cities Conference, Coventry Cathedral, Coventry, England, mimeographed

Pettigrew, Thomas F
    1964   *A Profile of the Negro American.* Princeton, New Jersey: Van Nostrand
    1973   Racism and the mental health of white Americans: a social psychological view, *in* Willie, Charles V; Kramer, Bernard M; and Brown, Bertram S (eds) *Racism and Mental Health.* Pittsburgh, Pennsylvania: University of Pittsburgh Press

Silberman, Charles E 1964 *Crisis in Black and White.* New York: Random House

Stark, Werner 1966 *The Sociology of Religion: A Study of Christendom,* vol 1, *Established Religions.* New York: Fordham University Press

Stonequist, Everett V 1937 *The Marginal Man.* New York: Scribner's

Tillich, Paul 1955 *Biblical Religion and the Search for Ultimate Reality.* Chicago, Ill: Univ of Chicago Press

Trilling, Lionel 1955 *The Opposing Self.* New York: Viking

U S Bureau of the Census 1972 *Census of Population: 1970, General Social and Economic Characteristics* (Final

U S Bureau of the Census *(cont)*
Report PC (1)—C1 United States). Washington, D C: U S
Government Printing Office
U S Department of Labor 1965 *The Negro Family.* Wash-
ington, D C: U S Government Printing Office
Williams, H C N 1968 *in* Willie, Charles V (1968) Sum-
mary of the Report of the People and Cities Conference,
Coventry Cathedral, Coventry, England, mimeographed
Williams, John A 1970 *The King God Didn't Save.* New
York: Coward-McCann
Willie, Charles V
  1967   (ed) *The Family Life of Black People.* Colum-
          bus, Ohio: Merrill
  1968   Summary of the Report of the People and Cities
          Conference, Coventry Cathedral, Coventry, Eng-
          land, mimeographed
  1969a   *Church Action in the World: Studies in Sociol-
          ogy and Religion.* New York: Morehouse-Barlow
  1969b   Intergenerational Poverty. *Poverty and Human
          Resources Abstracts* 4:11
  and Kramer, Bernard M, and Brown, Bertram S (eds)
          1973 *Racism and Mental Health.* Pittsburgh,
          Pennsylvania: University of Pittsburgh Press
  and Levy, Joan D 1972 Black is lonely. *Psychology
          Today* 5(10):50
  and McCord, Arline Sakuma 1972 *Black Students at
          White Colleges.* New York: Praeger
Wright, Richard, and Rosskan, Edwin 1941 *12 Million
Black Voices.* New York: Viking